CARROT HOUSE

New Get Up To Speed+ 3 Situational
© Carrot House

All rights reserved. No part of this publication may be reproduced,
stores in a retrieval system, or transmitted in any form or by any means
without the prior permission in writing of Carrot House.

Printed : First published January 2019
　　　　　Reprinted September 2019

Author : Carrot Language Lab

ISBN 978-89-6732-293-9

Printed and distributed in Korea
9F, 488, Gangnam St. Gangnam-gu, Seoul, 06120, South Korea

Curriculum Map

Course	Level 1	Level 2	Level 3	Level 4	Level 5	Level 6	Level 7
General Conversation	Essential English : Begin Again						
	Pre Get Up to Speed 1~2	New Get Up to Speed+ 1~2					
			New Get Up to Speed+ 3~4				
				New Get Up to Speed+ 5~6			
					New Get Up to Speed+ 7~8		
	Daily Focused English 1						
		Daily Focused English 2					
Discussion				Active Discussion 1			
					Active Discussion 2		
						Dynamic Discussion	
			Chicken Soup Course				
				Dynamic Information & Digital Technology			
Business Conversation	Pre Business Basics 1						
		Pre Business Basics 2					
			Business Basics 1				
				Business Basics 2			
					Business Practice 1		
						Business Practice 2	
Global Biz Workshop				Effective Business Writing Skills (Workbook)			
				Effective Presentation Skills (Workbook)			
					Effective Negotiation Skills (Workbook)		
					Cross-Cultural Training 1~2 (Workbook)		
					Leadership Training Course (Workbook)		
Business Skills				Simple & Clear Technical Writing Skills			
				Effective Business Writing Skills			
				Effective Meeting Skills			
				Business Communication (Negotiation)			
				Effective Presentation Skills			
					Marketing 1		
						Marketing 2	
						Management	
On the Job English				Human Resources			
				Accounting and Finance			
				Marketing and Sales			
				Production Management			
				Automotive			
				Banking and Commerce			
				Medical and Medicine			
				Information Technology			
				Construction			
			Construction English in Use 1 ~ 4				
			Public Service English in Use				

※ This Curriculum Map illustrates the entire line-up of textbooks at CARROT HOUSE.

CARROT HOUSE _ 2019.01

Introduction

Carrot House Methodology

Andragogical Approach & Productive English
The teaching of children (pedagogy) and adult learning (andragogy) are distinctively different. Pedagogy is akin to training and encourages convergent thinking and rote learning. It is compulsory, centered on the teacher and the imparting of information with minimal control by the learner. Andragogy, by contrast, is about education as freedom. It encourages divergent thinking and active learning. It is voluntary, learner oriented and opens up vistas for continual learning. Adults need to feel independent and in control of their learning. Therefore, Carrot House curriculum is based on andragogy and is designed to encourage learners' participation and engagement by providing more task-based activities and opportunities to frequently interact in the classroom. People want to achieve communicative competence when they learn other languages. English education in EFL environments has been rather focused on the receptive skills of English—listening and reading—which simply increases learners' knowledge about a language, not the competence of using it. If people are well equipped with productive skills—speaking and writing—they will be competent in English communication. This is why Carrot House curriculum is designed to enhance learners' productive skills throughout the course. This andragogical approach of the Carrot House Curriculum, which focuses on productive English, will enable learners to achieve communication skills necessary for global competence. Carrot House's teaching philosophy and curriculum combine to provide a "Language for Success" for all learners.

Communicative Language Learning (CLL)
This communicative interaction, the essential component of language acquisition, does not occur in a typical, non-meaningful, fun-oriented conversation with native speakers. It occurs in a negotiated interaction through which a well-trained teacher provides the comprehensible input that is appropriate to the learners. The learners, at the same time, actively utilize the opportunities given to them by the teachers. To this end, the Communicative Language Learning (CLL) method is employed in the field of Foreign Language Acquisition. The CLL method provides activities that are geared toward using language pragmatically, authentically and functionally with the intention of achieving meaningful purposes.

Course Overview

Features

Productive English
Learn to use practical and authentic expressions in various daily conversation, common collocations, written sentences, and activities.

Maximization of Schema
The use of visual texts, topic specific questions and useful expressions allow learners to find connections between the contents and their lives by maximizing their schema.

Interactive Activity
Activities, such as role-play, pair-work, group-work, and class-work, provide learners with the opportunity to constantly interact each other.

A Range of Everyday Topics
Through dealing with a range of daily situations in class, learners are equipped to tackle similar situations in reality.

Discussion
Learners can expand their ability to effectively express themselves in English through discussing a broad range of topics.

Slang / Idiom
Through learning topic-related slang and idioms, learners can improve their English language proficiency and use contemporary informal expressions to articulate their ideas.

Opinions on Topic-related Situations
Aims to enhance learner's abilities to speak logically. This task gives learners the chance to express their opinions on a given topic or from a choice of two situations.

Lesson Composition

Each New Get Up To Speed+ Situational book is composed of 12 lessons. Each lesson is composed of 7 main activities and 5 useful extra activities.

1. Warm Up Activity

To activate the students and their background knowledge, the lesson starts with discussing an image together with three situation-related-questions.

2. Useful Expression

Students can expand their English-language ability by practicing actively used expressions in various situations.

3. Key Conversation

Students can read, listen, and repeat how native speakers communicate with others on a daily basis. The activity also includes questions to test comprehension skills.

4. Language Practice

Students can practice using key words and expressions to complete sentences and create their own sentences. This helps students to apply and remember what they have learned.

Lesson Composition

Each New Get Up To Speed+ Situational book is composed of 12 lessons. Each lesson is composed of 7 main activities and 5 useful extra activities.

5. Role Plays

Task-based role plays puts off the burden of acting but focuses on the language and task achievement and ability to express oneself in various situations.

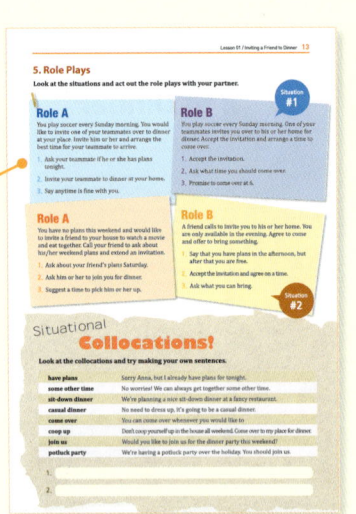

6. Cultural Discussion Questions

Gives the learners the opportunity to share, learn, and discuss global, cultural, and personal opinions and notions.

7. Slang & Idioms

Reinforce the learner's ability to speak English like a native through the use of situational contemporary slang & idioms.

Extra Activities

Each lesson includes five extra activities: three engaging facts and figures, Situational Collocations, and Did You Know?. These activities provides students with both popular and intriguing global facts. These can also be used to help facilitate a more fun and enjoyable class.

Contents

Title	Learning Objective	Expression Check	
Lesson 1 Inviting a Friend to Dinner	To invite a friend over to your house for dinner.	- Do you have any plans this weekend? - Would you like to come over for dinner? - What time works best for you?	10
Lesson 2 Getting Some New Wheels	To purchase a new car from a dealership.	- I'm in the market for a new car. - What make and model are you interested in? - What are the standard options?	16
Lesson 3 Let's Call It a Night	To end an evening out with friends.	- What do you say we call it a night? - It's getting to be that time of night. - I think it's time for me to head home.	22
Lesson 4 Choosing a Pet	To find a suitable family pet.	- We want a breed that is good with children. - Are they hard to housetrain? - Does she have all of her shots?	28
Lesson 5 Wedding Season	To congratulate a newly married couple.	- Congratulations on your big day! - Here comes the happy couple! - Wishing you many years of happiness together.	34
Lesson 6 A New Hobby	To discuss your pastimes and hobbies.	- Do you belong to any clubs? - We are forming a new club. - I didn't know you were into…	40
Lesson 7 What Do You Recommend?	To make recommendations to other people when ordering from a menu.	- I highly recommend getting the steak. - You should try the roast chicken. It's so good. - I'd definitely order that if I were you.	46
Lesson 8 Back to Work	To talk about your past weekend in detail.	- What did you do over the weekend? - I didn't get up to too much. - I was basically a couch potato all weekend.	52
Lesson 9 I Need to Cancel	To cancel a plan that you have made with someone.	- I'm really sorry, but I have to cancel our appointment. - It's no problem. Do you want to reschedule? - Unfortunately, something came up, and I have to cancel.	58
Lesson 10 Monthly Bills	To discuss paying monthly bills.	- I'd like to pay my monthly utility bill, please. - Can I pay my cell phone bill here as well? - That should make us even.	64
Lesson 11 Going to the Doctor	To visit a doctor and describe your symptoms.	- I don't feel very well today. - What are your symptoms? - I'll prescribe some medicine for you.	70
Lesson 12 The Highlight of My Trip	To discuss places you have traveled with others.	- Catch me up on your trip! - The highlight for me had to be seeing the Northern Lights. - I'll remember it forever.	76

Slang & Idioms — 82

Answer Key — 84

Inviting a Friend to Dinner

01 Inviting a Friend to Dinner

» Learning Objective

Upon completion of this lesson, you will be able to…

invite a friend over to your house for dinner.

» Expression Check

- ☑ Do you have any plans this weekend?
- ☑ Would you like to come over for dinner?
- ☑ What time works best for you?

1. Warm Up Activity

Describe what is happening in the picture.

Talk about the questions.

1. Which do you prefer - going out to dinner with a friend or eating at a friend's home? Why?
2. Do you often get invited to friends' homes for dinner? Explain.
3. Tell about the last time that you invited a friend to your house. What did you do?

2. Useful Expressions

Match the expressions (a-d) to its similar meaning (1-4).

A. What are you up to this weekend?

B. How about letting me cook you dinner on Saturday?

C. How does six o'clock sound to you?

D. When should I pick you up?

1. Does six o'clock suit you?

2. When would you like me to get you?

3. Do you have any plans this weekend?

4. Would you like to come over for dinner on Saturday?

3. Key Conversation

🎧 **Think of the useful expressions and practice the dialogue.**

How About Dinner?

Lisa	Hey, how's your day going?
Linda	Not too bad, but I can't wait for it to be over.
Lisa	Do you have any plans this weekend?
Linda	Nothing special. Why do you ask?
Lisa	Would you like to come over to my place for dinner on Saturday?
Linda	I'd love to. What time on Saturday?
Lisa	It doesn't matter to me. What time works best for you?
Linda	How does six o'clock sound to you?
Lisa	Should I pick you up around 5:30?
Linda	Perfect, I'll be ready. What can I bring?
Lisa	Nothing. I'll take care of everything.

Questions

1. Do you think Linda is having a good day? Why?

2. Do you think this is the first time they have made plans together?

3. Do you think Lisa is busy on Saturday?

4. Do you think Linda is going to enjoy herself?

Inviting a Friend to Dinner

Top Three Table Manners to Remember:

1. Unfold your napkin and place it on your lap.
   - Use it for wiping your lips or fingers.
   - At the end of dinner, leave the napkin neatly folded on the place setting.

2. If there are several different pieces of cutlery beside the plate, start at the outside.

3. When eating, rest your knife and fork on either side of the plate between mouthfuls. When you are finished, place them side-by-side in the center of the plate.

Q. When was the last time you were invited to a dinner party?

4. Language Practice

Using the key words, complete the sentences then practice making your own sentences.

Practice #1 — Asking about plans	Practice #2 — Extending an invitation	Practice #3 — Arranging a time
• next weekend • after work • Saturday night	• come over for dinner • getting together • having a bite	• six o'clock • half past five • around 9
★ What are you up to _____?	★ How about _____ to eat at my place?	★ Does _____ suit you?
★ Are you doing anything _____?	★ Would you like to _____?	★ Would you be okay with coming _____?
★ Do you have any plans _____?	★ What do you think about _____ at my house?	★ How does _____ sound to you?

5. Role Plays

Look at the situations and act out the role plays with your partner.

Situation #1

Role A
You play soccer every Sunday morning. You would like to invite one of your teammates over to dinner at your place. Invite him or her and arrange the best time for your teammate to arrive.

1. Ask your teammate if he or she has plans tonight.
2. Invite your teammate to dinner at your home.
3. Say anytime is fine with you.

Role B
You play soccer every Sunday morning. One of your teammates invites you over to his or her home for dinner. Accept the invitation and arrange a time to come over.

1. Accept the invitation.
2. Ask what time you should come over.
3. Promise to come over at 6.

Role A
You have no plans this weekend and would like to invite a friend to your house to watch a movie and eat together. Call your friend to ask about his/her weekend plans and extend an invitation.

1. Ask about your friend's plans Saturday.
2. Ask him or her to join you for dinner.
3. Suggest a time to pick him or her up.

Role B
A friend calls to invite you to his or her home. You are only available in the evening. Agree to come and offer to bring something.

1. Say that you have plans in the afternoon, but after that you are free.
2. Accept the invitation and agree on a time.
3. Ask what you can bring.

Situation #2

Situational Collocations!

Look at the collocations and try making your own sentences.

have plans	Sorry Anna, but I already have plans for tonight.
some other time	No worries! We can always get together some other time.
sit-down dinner	We're planning a nice sit-down dinner at a fancy restaurant.
casual dinner	No need to dress up, it's going to be a casual dinner.
come over	You can come over whenever you would like to
coop up	Don't coop yourself up in the house all weekend. Come over to my place for dinner.
join us	Would you like to join us for the dinner party this weekend?
potluck party	We're having a potluck party over the holiday. You should join us.

1.
2.

Inviting a Friend to Dinner

Difficult Dinner Guests and 3 Delicious Meals to Feed Them

THE 5 MOST CHALLENGING DINNER GUESTS EVER
VEGAN
GLUTEN INTOLERANT
ALLERGIC TO EGGS
ALLERGIC TO NUTS
LACTOSE INTOLERANT

3 Meals to Feed Nearly Anyone

1. Mushroom Risotto with Caramelized Onions
Vegan, gluten-free, full of flavor

2. Braised Coconut Spinach and Chickpeas with Lemon
A deeply delicious stew, vibrant and colorful

3. Soba Noodle Salad with Bok Choy
Make sure to use gluten-free soba noodles in this fresh soba dish

Q1. Have you ever prepared food for guests? How did you choose what to cook?

Q2. What are the most popular dishes to serve at a dinner party in your country? Explain.

6. Cultural Discussion Questions

Talk about the questions in as much detail as possible.

1. Do you think having a home-cooked meal is better than going out to eat at a restaurant?

2. What are some special occasions when it is popular to invite others over for a meal in your country? What do you do to prepare?

3. Do you prefer to cook familiar food when cooking for others, or would you rather try new recipes? Explain.

4. Do you think it is more expensive to have people over for dinner or to go out?

Did You Know?

Read and discuss how you feel about each fact.

1. Did you know that researchers have found that *beer helps prevent* the growth of bacteria that leads to *tooth decay* and *gum disease*?

2. Did you know that a Harvard study found that people who ate *spicy food* often had a *14 percent lower risk of death* than people who only ate spicy foods once a week?

7. Slang & Idioms

Match the slang phrases and idioms with their definitions and use them to complete the sentences below.

1. ___ show up empty-handed
2. ___ eating me out of house and home
3. ___ feed an army
4. ___ a spread
5. ___ could eat a horse

A. to eat so much as to deplete someone's resources
B. a large and impressively elaborate meal
C. to have a lot of food
D. to be extremely hungry
E. without bringing anything

1. You've really outdone yourself this time. You prepared quite _____.
2. I need to go to the grocery store again. My kids are _____.
3. When's dinner? I'm so hungry I _____.
4. We have enough food at this potluck dinner to _____.
5. You should bring a bottle of wine with you. It's important to never _____.

Wrapping Up!

Write down four things you learned from this lesson and review.

1. _____
2. _____
3. _____
4. _____

Getting Some New Wheels

02 Getting Some New Wheels

» **Learning Objective**

Upon completion of this lesson, you will be able to...

purchase a new car from a dealership.

» **Expression Check**

- ☑ I'm in the market for a new car.
- ☑ What make and model are you interested in?
- ☑ What are the standard options?

1. Warm Up Activity

Describe what is happening in the picture.

Talk about the questions.

1. Do you have a car? If you do, please describe it.
2. What features do you think are most important when buying a new car? Be specific.
3. What is your dream car?

2. Useful Expressions

Match the expressions (a-d) to its similar meaning (1-4).

A I'd like a car with all the options.

B I need a fuel-efficient vehicle.

C What are the standard features?

D Could you come down a little off the sticker price?

1 What is usually included?

2 Will you give me a discount?

3 I want one that has every luxury feature.

4 I'd like a car that has a good fuel economy rating.

3. Key Conversation

Think of the useful expressions and practice the dialogue.

I Need a New Ride

Salesman	Hi, ma'am, may I help you?
Maddie	Yes, thanks. I'm in the market for a new car.
Salesman	What type of vehicle do you have in mind?
Maddie	I'm looking for something kind of sporty and compact that gets good gas mileage.
Salesman	I definitely have some great cars that fit the bill. Are you interested in any particular make or model?
Maddie	I'm open to suggestions, but I heard that the new Hondas have excellent safety ratings, so I'd like to start there.
Salesman	Sure. This model is an excellent choice. It has great fuel economy and it's a bestseller this month.
Maddie	It's really comfortable and actually quite roomy. The center console is nice, and I love the rearview camera.
Salesman	That comes standard, but we also have an optional GPS.
Maddie	I'll have to see how it handles on the road, but I think I really like the feel of this one.

Questions

1. What kind of car would you recommend for Maddie?
2. Do you think it is a good idea for Maddie to get the GPS offered by the salesman?
3. Why is it important to take a vehicle for a test drive before making a purchase?
4. Do you think it is necessary to read car reviews before purchasing a car?

Getting Some New Wheels

What Do You Call This?

Sometimes, incorrect English words and expressions can be adopted into other languages. Guess what the correct terms are for these three car parts.

Useful Expressions

1 *at the wheel*
She fell asleep at the wheel of her car.

2 *honk the horn*
Honking your horn excessively can cause unnecessary distractions.

3 *change lanes*
It is difficult to change lanes in a truck in heavy traffic.

Not "Front Window" 1
Not "Back Mirror" 2
Not "Handle" 3

Answer: (1) Windshield (2) Side-view mirror (3) Steering wheel

4. Language Practice

Using the key words, complete the sentences then practice making your own sentences.

Practice #1 — Options

- rearview camera
- customize / interior
- GPS

★ What can I do to _____ the _____?

★ Does a _____ come installed?

★ I really want a built-in _____ .

Practice #2 — Features

- manual transmission
- air conditioning
- gas mileage

★ What kind of _____ does this model get?

★ I've got to have _____ _____ in my new car.

★ Does it come in a _____?

Practice #3 — Making a deal

- any extras
- give a discount
- cut a deal

★ I'm ready to _____.

★ I can _____ if you pay in cash.

★ Can you throw in _____?

Lesson 02 / Getting Some New Wheels

5. Role Plays

Look at the situations and act out the role plays with your partner.

Situation #1

Role A
You are buying your first car. You want a basic fuel-efficient vehicle at the best price possible.

1. Tell the salesperson about your needs.
2. You are not interested in paying extra for options.
3. Ask to test drive a compact car.

Role B
You are a salesperson at an auto dealership. Your customer is interested in buying something practical with good gas mileage. Recommend one of the new compact cars you have in stock.

1. Ask about the customer's driving habits.
2. Check what options the customer is interested in.
3. Ask what size of car the customer is interested in. Suggest a compact car.

Situation #2

Role A
You are a salesperson at a car dealership. A customer is interested in upgrading to a larger vehicle. Tell the customer about your new family-friendly SUVs.

1. Ask about the customer's needs.
2. Ask if the customer is interested in any specific options.
3. Suggest an SUV.

Role B
You just had your second child. You need to upgrade to a larger car and are interested in models that offer special features for children. You want the most comfortable car possible for your growing family.

1. Tell about your family.
2. Ask if there are any features that are good for children.
3. Ask about the gas mileage.

Situational Collocations!

Look at the collocations and try making your own sentences.

break down	This car is old and apt to break down.
used car	My husband changed his mind and bought a used car.
heavy traffic	The snowstorm is causing heavy traffic all over the city.
wide selection	Why not stop by and look at the wide selection offered?
fill up	I need to fill up the tank.
rush-hour	I need to leave early just to avoid rush-hour.
pull over	I had to pull over because I ran out of gas.
tire went flat	My tire went flat on the highway.

1.
2.

Getting Some New Wheels

Names Matter

General Motors (GM) had a problem when they introduced the Chevy Nova in South America. Despite their best efforts, they were not selling many cars.

They finally realized that, in Spanish, **"Nova"** means **"It doesn't go."** Sales improved dramatically after the car was renamed the **"Caribe."**

6. Cultural Discussion Questions

Talk about the questions in as much detail as possible.

1. What kinds of cars are most popular in your country? Why?
2. Where do most people buy cars in your country? Explain.
3. Do people in your country think it is better to buy a new or used car? Why?
4. How do you find the best deal for a car where you live?

Did You Know?

Read and discuss how you feel about each fact.

1. Did you know that the average price of a new car in the US is **$32,169**?
2. Did you know that a new car usually **loses 25-40%** of its value within the first two years?

Different Types of Cars

According to a survey, 39% of respondents preferred compact cars, followed by mid-sized sedans at 20% and SUVs at 16%.

Q. Which type of car do you prefer? Why?

- Others 15%
- Compact 39%
- Sports car 10%
- SUV 16%
- Mid Size 20%

SUV (Sport Utility Vehicle) VS. Compact Car

7. Slang & Idioms

Match the slang phrases and idioms with their definitions and use them to complete the sentences below.

1. ___ for a spin
2. ___ carpool
3. ___ put the pedal to the metal
4. ___ drove a hard bargain
5. ___ fully loaded

A. to drive as fast as possible
B. with all the options
C. an arrangement between people to make a regular journey in a single vehicle
D. to test or try out something, especially an automobile
E. to be uncompromising in making a deal

1. He really _____, but I think we got a good deal.
2. I wish I could afford a _____ car.
3. Rally drivers need to _____.
4. Before I make a final decision, I'll need to take the car _____.
5. We're going to the same place. Why don't we _____?

Wrapping Up!
Write down four things you learned from this lesson and review.

1 2 3 4

Let's Call It a Night

03

Let's Call It a Night

» **Learning Objective**

Upon completion of this lesson, you will be able to...
end an evening out with friends.

» **Expression Check**

- ☑ What do you say we call it a night?
- ☑ It's getting to be that time of night.
- ☑ I think it's time for me to head home.

1. Warm Up Activity

Describe what is happening in the picture.

Talk about the questions.

1. Would you rather be the first to leave a party or the last? Explain.
2. What kinds of excuses do you give when leaving a gathering early?
3. How do you say no when you have had enough to drink?

2. Useful Expressions

Match the expressions (a-d) to its similar meaning (1-4).

- **A** Let's call it a night.
- **B** I've got to go home and sleep it off.
- **C** I've got an early morning tomorrow.
- **D** It's getting a little late for me.

- **1** I'll feel better after I get some sleep.
- **2** I'm tired and I'm ready to go home.
- **3** I've got to wake up early.
- **4** Let's go home.

3. Key Conversation

🎧 **Think of the useful expressions and practice the dialogue.**

Bailing Early

Ken	Hey, can I get one more round of drinks over here, please?
Derek	No, no–I'm slowing down, Ken. It's already midnight.
Ken	Come on, you aren't wussing out on me, are you?
Derek	It's not that...I just have to crawl out of bed by 6:00 tomorrow for that meeting.
Ken	I'll let you off this time, but you owe me next time, OK?
Derek	You're on. Sorry to have to bail so early, but don't leave on my account!
Ken	I won't! Well, it looks like Josh has had enough, too. I guess it's time to call it a night.
Derek	I'll see you guys at the office after lunch.
Ken	Yeah, go sleep it off. I don't want to get blamed if your presentation is lousy tomorrow.
Derek	Ha ha. Thanks for the support!

Questions

1. Do you think Derek did the right thing by going home before his co-workers?
2. Do you think Ken wants to go home?
3. What would you say to Derek if you really wanted him to stay and drink with you?
4. Do you think the three men will be OK for work in the morning?

Let's Call It a Night

Drinking Etiquette Around the World

West
Toasting in Sweden involves eye contact but no glass-touching. A "skol" and a nod to everyone will do the trick.

East
When you drink Chinese liquor, baiju, drink with restraint. Draining your glass will result in a refill. If you do not want more, leave the glass half-full.

Q1. What is the most common toast (the equivalent of "cheers") in your country?
Q2. Tell us about toasting etiquette in your country.

4. Language Practice

Using the key words, complete the sentences then practice making your own sentences.

Practice #1 — Leaving
- bail
- head for home
- take off

★ Sorry, but I'd better _____.

★ I've got to _____ in a few minutes.

★ I need to _____. Sorry!

Practice #2 — Finishing
- call it a night
- close out my tab
- shut things down

★ I think it's time to _____.

★ I've got to _____.

★ Time to _____ guys!

Practice #3 — Accepting an excuse
- make it up to me
- No worries.
- Go sleep it off.

★ _____. It's getting late.

★ You can _____ next time.

★ _____. We'll talk again soon.

5. Role Plays

Look at the situations and act out the role plays with your partner.

Situation #1

Role A

You just had dinner with your coworkers and they want to go to another bar. You promised your spouse that you would come home early to help with something. Make an excuse and leave.

1. Tell your coworkers that you are leaving.
2. Explain why you are leaving.
3. Promise to make it up to your coworkers next time.

Role B

You are a team leader. You have permission to use the company credit card to take your staff out to dinner and drinks tonight. One of your employees wants to go home early. Try to persuade him or her to stay out a little longer.

1. Ask if he or she can stay for one more drink.
2. Insist that it won't be for a long time.
3. Accept your employee's excuse and say it is okay.

Situation #2

Role A

You are drinking with your best friend. You usually have to work early, but you have tomorrow off. You don't get to stay out late very often and you to have a few more drinks.

1. Offer to buy the next round.
2. Try to persuade your friend to stay out a little longer.
3. Agree to leave and ask your friend to meet again soon.

Role B

You are having drinks with your best friend. Your friend wants to order another round. Politely explain you need to go home early because you have work tomorrow.

1. Tell your friend that you have to go.
2. Explain why you need to leave.
3. Promise to buy your friend a drink next time.

Situational Collocations!

Look at the collocations and try making your own sentences.

wrap up	I want to wrap up this deal as quickly as possible.
head home	Let's grab a beer to unwind before we head home.
swing by	Would you swing by my place after you're done with work?
running late	The bus is running late than usual.
hang out	That was fun! Let's hang out again soon.
sign off	I'm going to sign off now.
get going	I should probably get going.
farewell party	We threw him a farewell party before he left.

1. ....

2. ....

Let's Call It a Night

What Kind of *Alcohol Do People Drink?*

Alcoholic drinks are drank worldwide, but how much and what kind? Below is a graph or how much alcohol nations drink and what kind of alcohol they prefer.

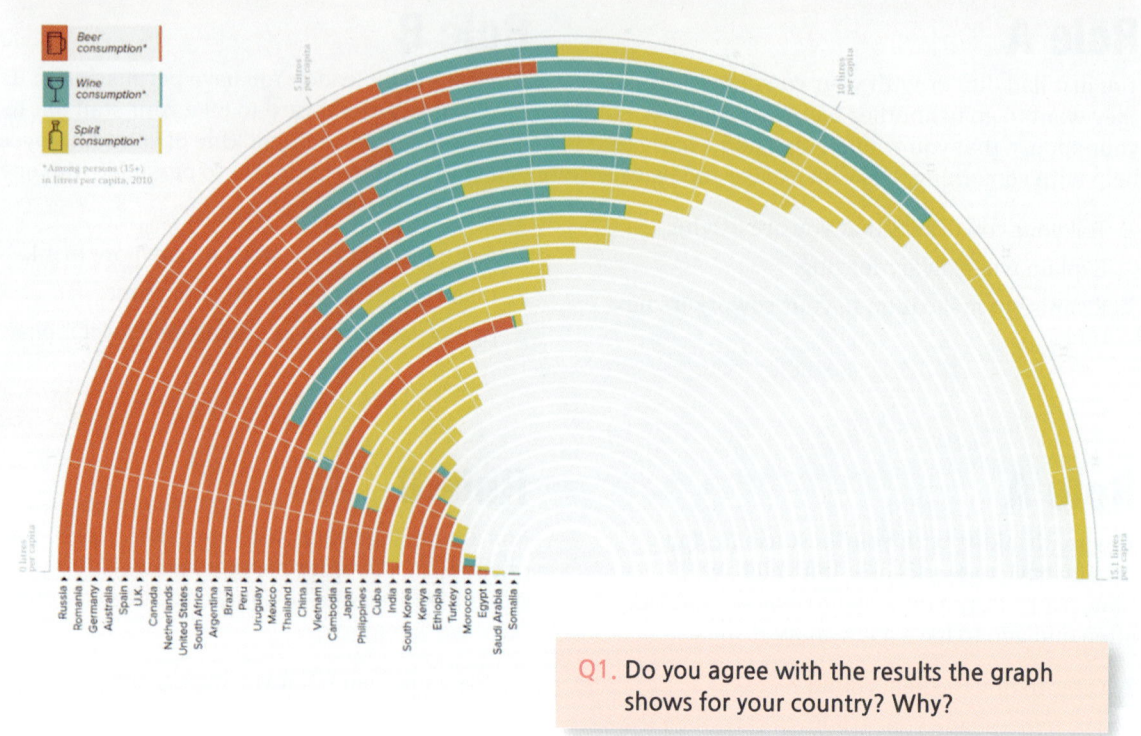

Q1. Do you agree with the results the graph shows for your country? Why?

6. Cultural Discussion Questions

Talk about the questions in as much detail as possible.

1. Do you often stay out late during the work week? Why?
2. In your culture, is it rude to say no when someone offers you a drink? Explain.
3. How do you usually return home from a late night?
4. In your office, is it acceptable to come to work hung over?

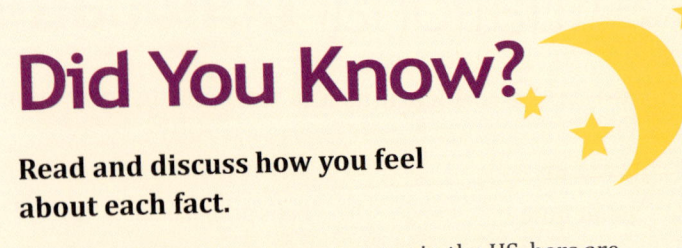

Did You Know?

Read and discuss how you feel about each fact.

1. Did you know that in most states in the US, bars are legally required to **stop serving alcohol** at a certain time (most commonly **2:00 a.m.**)?

2. Did you know in Thailand alcohol cannot be sold between **midnight to 11:00 a.m.** and **2:00 p.m. to 5:00 p.m.**!?

Best Alcohol-Food Pairings

Do you enjoy having a snack while you drink? Although there are no strict rules for what to eat with certain drinks, finding the right pairing can result in an improved dining experience. Raise a toast to the dishes that bring out your drink's optimal flavor.

Beer
+
Which food?

Red Wine
+
Which food?

Q1. Which foods do you think pair best with beer and red wine?

Q2. What are some traditional alcoholic beverages in your country? What types of food go best with them?

7. Slang & Idioms

Match the slang phrases and idioms with their definitions and use them to complete the sentences below.

1. ___ hit the road   A. to have to go
2. ___ split   B. to stop what you have been doing and go home
3. ___ call it a night   C. an event or task that continues throughout the night
4. ___ hit the sack   D. to leave a place
5. ___ all-nighter   E. to go to bed

1. I can't pull an _____ today.

2. Time to _____, everyone! Bye! See you next time.

3. Well, it's pretty late. It's time for us to _____, guys!

4. I think I'm going to _____ now. I have to get up early tomorrow.

5. I'd better go and _____. I'm pretty tired.

Wrapping Up!

Write down four things you learned from this lesson and review.

1. _____
2. _____
3. _____
4. _____

Choosing a Pet

04

» **Learning Objective**

Upon completion of this lesson, you will be able to...
find a suitable family pet.

» **Expression Check**

- ☑ We want a breed that is good with children.
- ☑ Are they hard to housetrain?
- ☑ Does she have all of her shots?

1. Warm Up Activity

Describe what is happening in the picture.

Talk about the questions.

1. What kinds of pets have you had in the past?
2. Which animals are the most popular pets in your country? Why do you think that is?
3. What do you think are the most important factors to consider when selecting a new pet?

2. Useful Expressions

Match the expressions (a-d) to its similar meaning (1-4).

- **A** We want a breed that is good with children.
- **B** Are they hard to housetrain?
- **C** Does she have all of her shots?
- **D** Is he fixed?

- **1** Has she gotten all of her vaccines?
- **2** We'd like a breed that's known to be kid-friendly.
- **3** Has he been neutered?
- **4** Are they hard to teach to use the bathroom?

3. Key Conversation

Think of the useful expressions and practice the dialogue.

A New Friend

Melinda	I've had my heart set on getting a Yorkie for a long time.
Clerk	Well, it looks like he's already made up his mind about you!
Melinda	I've heard they bark a lot though and I live in an apartment, so I'm worried about my neighbors.
Clerk	It's true that they are good watch dogs, but they can be taught to be quiet.
Melinda	Are they hard to housetrain?
Clerk	No. Many people just use training pads in the house to start off with, and then walks as they get older.
Melinda	Does he have all his shots?
Clerk	Yes, he's had his rabies and all his basic puppy immunizations.
Melinda	Great! What about getting him fixed?
Clerk	We have an in-house vet you can schedule that with.
Melinda	Thanks for all your help. He's going to make a great addition to the family.

Questions

1. Do you think Melinda has thought a lot about buying a Yorkie?
2. Do you think the salesclerk reassured Melinda well about her questions?
3. What other questions do you think Melinda should ask the sales clerk about her new friend?
4. Do you think a dog would make a good pet for an apartment-dweller?

Choosing a Pet

Benefits of Pet Ownership

According to a survey, 92% of the respondents indicated that they derive significant health benefits from their pets.

Anyone who has ever loved a pet knows how much joy that relationship can bring. There is increasing scientific evidence that the unique bond we share with our pets dramatically enriches our lives, our physical health, and our emotional well-being. Pets can help to reduce stress, relieve loneliness and depression, prevent heart disease, and lower healthcare costs.

Some studies showed:

- *People with hypertension* – have lower blood pressure in stressful situations
- *People without cats* – are between 30% and 40% more likely to die of cardiovascular disease
- *Older people who have pets* – experience better physical health and mental well-being
- *People with pets* – make fewer doctor visits, especially for non-serious medical conditions
- *Heart patients who owned pets* – had a better chance of long-term survival than patients who did not own pets

4. Language Practice

Using the key words, complete the sentences then practice making your own sentences.

Practice #1 — Types

- breeds
- temperament
- size

★ How would you describe its usual _____?

★ What _____ will it be when it is fully-grown?

★ What _____ of cat do you have for sale?

Practice #2 — Care instructions

- feed
- exercise
- health issues

★ Are there any _____ that I should be aware of?

★ How much _____ will it need and how often?

★ How much should I _____ it?

Practice #3 — Requirements

- relatively quiet / apartment
- independent / work late
- low maintenance / busy schedule

★ I need a pet that's _____ since I usually _____.

★ Our family is looking for a _____ pet since we have such a _____ these days.

★ I'd like a pet that's _____ _____ since I live in an _____.

5. Role Plays

Look at the situations and act out the role plays with your partner.

Situation #1

Role A

Your family has decided to adopt a dog from a local animal shelter. You see an adorable dog, but you have some questions about its basic care. Talk to a worker before making your decision.

1. Ask what size the dog will grow to.
2. Check if the dog has any special needs (food, exercise, etc.).
3. Confirm that the dog is good with children.

Role B

You are a volunteer at an animal shelter. A family is interested in one of the dogs. It's a fully-grown cocker spaniel mix. The dog is in good health and just needs to be walked twice a day. It is good with children and is already housetrained.

1. Tell the family that the dog is fully-grown.
2. Explain how often the dog needs to be walked.
3. Assure the family that the dog is good with children.

Situation #2

Role A

You are a breeder selling Siamese cats. A customer calls to ask you some questions. Your cats are intelligent, people-friendly, and calm. They are in good health and are 8 to 15 pounds when fully-grown.

1. Ask if the customer has any questions.
2. Explain about the cats' characteristics and health.
3. Ask if the customer is interested in seeing the cats in person.

Role B

You are interested in buying a Siamese cat but aren't sure if it is the best pet for a small apartment. Talk about your concerns with a breeder.

1. Ask about the cats' health and temperament.
2. Find out if the cats are good in apartments.
3. Make an appointment to come and pick out a cat. prepare.

Situational Collocations!

Look at the collocations and try making your own sentences.

regular checkup	Regular checkup is a must for your pet care.
off limit	Many public facilities are off limit to animals.
pure breed	My dog is a pure breed.
tropical fish	My dad loves caring for his tropical fish.
chew up	My dog chewed up my shoes.
street cat	It's very kind of you to take care of a street cat!
shedding cycle	Our dog is going through a shedding cycle. There is fur everywhere!
lap dog	My grandparents adopted a lap dog.

1.
2.

Choosing a Pet

World's Most EXOTIC PETS

Many people apt for dogs and cats as their furry partners, but some people would prefer something more out of the ordinary. Not all exotic pets are legal in all regions, but in places where they can, people pay a hefty price to keep one.

#1 Ayam Cemani Chicken - $5,000
These chickens are completely black from feathers, to beak, to even bones and organs.

#2 Stag Beetle - $8,900
These majestic beetles can grow as large as 12cm.

#3 Toucan - $8,000
Very good-natured but high-maintenance because of their sensitive diet and need for large space.

#4 Savannah Cat - $12,000~$20,000
Affectionate and sweet-tempered cats. Very social, curious, and have high energy.

#5 De Brazza Monkey - $10,000 ~ $15,000
Most expensive monkeys in the world. They may look like wise old men, but are extremely shy animals.

6. Cultural Discussion Questions

Talk about the questions in as much detail as possible.

1. In your country, are pets welcomed in public spaces? Are there any places that they are not allowed?

2. Some people would argue that it is cruel and unnatural to keep animals as pets. Do you agree or disagree?

3. Many people consider their pets to be members of the family. What do you think about this?

4. If you could have any pet, what animal would you want? Why?

Did You Know?

Read and discuss how you feel about each fact.

1. Did you know that *21%* of pet dogs in the US were adopted from animal shelters?

2. Did you know that *33%* of households in the US own at least one cat and *39%* own at least one dog?

39% **33%**

How Much Do You Spend on Your Pets?

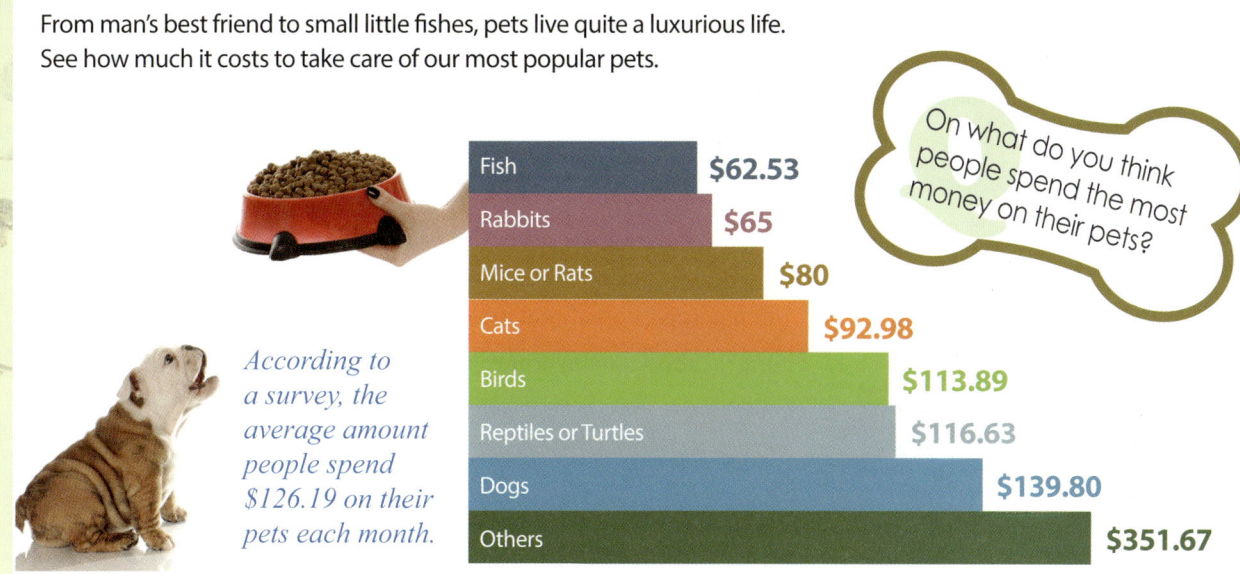

7. Slang & Idioms

Match the slang phrases and idioms with their definitions and use them to complete the sentences below.

1. ___ dog days
2. ___ working like a dog
3. ___ fighting like cats and dogs
4. ___ let the cat out of the bag
5. ___ dog-eat-dog

A. to work extremely hard
B. to fight and argue a lot
C. the hottest period of the year
D. a situation in which there is fierce, ruthless competition
E. reveal a secret carelessly or by mistake

1. It's a _____ world. The worse you act the better you make out.
2. The second I take my eyes off the kids, they start _____.
3. You _____. You've completely ruined the surprise.
4. The _____ of summer make me crave ice cream cones.
5. He's been _____ all week, so I hope he gets some down time soon.

Wrapping Up!

Write down four things you learned from this lesson and review.

05 Wedding Season

» Learning Objective

Upon completion of this lesson, you will be able to...

congratulate a newly married couple.

» Expression Check

- ☑ Congratulations on your big day!
- ☑ Here comes the happy couple!
- ☑ Wishing you many years of happiness together.

1. Warm Up Activity

Describe what is happening in the picture.

Talk about the questions.

1. What is the busiest time of year for weddings in your country?
2. What honeymoon destinations are most popular in your country?
3. How do wedding guests usually congratulate the bride and groom in your country?

2. Useful Expressions

Match the expressions (a-d) to its similar meaning (1-4).

- **A** Congratulations on your big day!
- **B** Here comes the happy couple.
- **C** I hope you guys enjoy a long life together.
- **D** So, you've finally tied the knot!

- **1** The bride and groom have arrived.
- **2** Congrats on your wedding!
- **3** Can't believe you guys are hitched now!
- **4** Wishing you many years of happiness together.

3. Key Conversation

Think of the useful expressions and practice the dialogue.

Finally Hitched!

Susan: Aww, you look so beautiful, Jane! Congratulations on your big day!

Jane: Thanks so much for coming! It's great to see you and everyone.

Susan: The whole ceremony was just so perfect, and the food is divine.

Jane: Well, I'm absolutely floating on air. Nothing could make this day any better for us!

Susan: So, you've finally tied the knot after all this time. I always knew you and Ashton were perfect for each other.

Jane: My parents would have been shocked if we hadn't after all these years of being joined at the hip!

Susan: Well, Alex and I wanted to give you a little something.

Jane: You didn't have to! Wow, cruise tickets?

Susan: It's not every day my best friend gets married, right?

Jane: Well, thanks so much! This is incredible!

Susan: I know you'll have fun. Wishing you many years of happiness!

Questions

1. Is Susan happy about her friend's marriage?
2. What makes a wedding memorable?
3. Do you think cruise tickets are a good wedding gift?
4. What would you give your best friend for a wedding present?

Wedding Season

Why Does the Bride Throw the Bouquet at Her Wedding?

Dating back to the 14th century, wedding guests in Western Europe tried to tear off bits of the bride's dress with the desire to take home a piece of the bride's luck. It was believed that the keepsake would bring good luck in love. People would chase after the lucky woman in the hope of a scrap of cloth or ribbon.

Of course, brides were opposed to the idea of being chased and having their wedding garments destroyed. As a result, the idea of distracting the crowd by throwing the bouquet emerged.

It became traditional for the bride to throw her bouquet at the reception and for all single women present to compete to catch it. The woman who catches the bouquet is said to be the next who will marry.

 Are there any unique traditions at wedding ceremonies in your country?

4. Language Practice

Using the key words, complete the sentences then practice making your own sentences.

Practice #1 — Discussing the ceremony

- get hitched
- tie the knot
- take the plunge

★ I'm so happy that you guys finally decided to _____!

★ They finally _____ after five years together!

★ I can't believe that you two finally _____!

Practice #2 — Offering congratulations

- marriage
- union
- the start of your life together

★ I wish you the best of luck in your _____!

★ Congratulations on your _____!

★ I'm so happy to be here to wish you luck with _____!

Practice #3 — Presenting a gift

- money
- present
- belated gift

★ I'm sorry that we couldn't make it to your wedding. We got you this _____ that we hope you'll appreciate.

★ I hope you enjoy this _____, but if not, please feel free to exchange it.

★ I wanted to give you some _____ to help you with your wedding expenses.

5. Role Plays

Look at the situations and act out the role plays with your partner.

Situation #1

Role A
You are about to get married. Your boss asks to come to speak with you about your wedding. You see that he is carrying a large box. You are excited but you do not think that you should accept such a large gift.

1. Thank your boss for the gift.
2. Say that the gift is too large and that you don't think you should keep it.
3. Accept the gift and thank your boss.

Role B
You are the manager of a small office. One of your employees is about to get married. You won't be able to attend the ceremony, so you decided to buy the couple a special present instead.

1. Congratulate your employee on his or her marriage.
2. Explain that you will not be attending the wedding and wanted to give him or her a special gift.
3. Insist that your employee accept the gift.

Situation #2

Role A
You are the best friend of the groom or bride. You want to congratulate your friend on his or her wedding day.

1. Congratulate your friend.
2. Tell about your favorite part of the ceremony.
3. Offer to take your friend out to dinner when he or she returns from the honeymoon.

Role B
You just got married. Talk to your best friend after the ceremony.

1. Thank your friend for coming.
2. Tell about how happy you feel.
3. Make plans to catch up when you return from your honeymoon.

Situational Collocations!

Look at the collocations and try making your own sentences.

special occasion	We would like to invite you to our special occasion.
wedding ring/ band	Emily showed off her beautiful wedding ring to her friends.
warm compliments	Thank you for your warm compliments.
perfect match	They are a perfect match for each other.
take place	The wedding is to take place during spring.
wedding anniversary	The Coles took off a day to celebrate their wedding anniversary.
make a toast	I would like to make a toast to the bride and groom.
big day	Tomorrow is the big day! You're getting married!

1. ....

2. ....

Wedding Season

Famous Wedding Quotes

Read the following quotes about marriage and discuss what you think they mean.

Success in marriage does not come merely through finding the right mate, but through being the right mate. ~Barnett R. Brickner

A long marriage is two people trying to dance a duet and two solos at the same time. ~Anne Taylor Fleming

Marriage is a book of which the first chapter is written in poetry and the remaining chapters in prose. ~Beverley Nichols

A successful marriage requires falling in love many times, always with the same person. ~Mignon McLaughlin

Marriage is an alliance entered into by a man who can't sleep with the window shut, and a woman who can't sleep with the window open. ~George Bernard Shaw

Happy marriages begin when we marry the ones we love, and they blossom when we love the ones we marry. ~Tom Mullen

6. Cultural Discussion Questions

Talk about the questions in as much detail as possible.

1. Tell about the most memorable wedding that you have ever attended. Where did it take place? What was so special about it?
2. What do people usually give as wedding gifts in your country?
3. What do guests usually wear to weddings in your country? Explain.
4. Where do weddings usually take place in your country?

Did You Know?

Read and discuss how you feel about each fact.

1. Did you know that **money is the number one** recommended **wedding gift**?
2. Did you know that, in the US, many couples **register for gifts at a retail store**? An expensive item from their registry would be considered a dream gift.

Lesson 05 / Wedding Season   39

Bridal Shower

A bridal shower is **a gift-giving party for a bride-to-be before her wedding.** Traditionally, the bridal shower is attended by **bridesmaids**, but today, a mixed "Jack and Jill" party attended by both men and women is also common.

Who are Bridesmaids?

The bridesmaids are members of the bride's party in a wedding. A bridesmaid is typically a young woman who is a close friend or sister of the bride. Bridesmaids customarily host the bridal shower.

Bachelor Party

A bachelor party is usually arranged by the groomsmen or the groom's male family members **to celebrate the groom's last days of freedom as a single man.** While there are no set rules concerning the events of a bachelor party, the evening is generally filled with males bonding over alcohol.

7. Slang & Idioms

Match the slang phrases and idioms with their definitions and use them to complete the sentences below.

1. ___ honeymoon period
2. ___ match made in heaven
3. ___ lovebirds
4. ___ apple of my eye
5. ___ head over heels

A. an openly affectionate couple.
B. a happy time at the start of a new relationship
C. to be madly in love
D. the one you love the most
E. a couple who gets along perfectly

1. Those two _____ are inseparable these days.
2. Sachi and Mark are a _____.
3. I don't expect we'll be hearing much from them during their _____.
4. Just looking at them, it's obvious that they are _____ in love with each other.
5. Mark is the _____ and I will cherish him.

Wrapping Up!
Write down four things you learned from this lesson and review.

1   2   3   4

06 A New Hobby

» **Learning Objective**

Upon completion of this lesson, you will be able to...
discuss your pastimes and hobbies.

» **Expression Check**

- ☑ Do you belong to any clubs?
- ☑ We are forming a new club.
- ☑ I didn't know you were into ...

1. Warm Up Activity

Describe what is happening in the picture.

Talk about the questions.

1. Have you ever joined a club? If so, what was it?
2. What kind of hobbies and pastimes do you enjoy?
3. Do you prefer hobbies that you can do on your own or those that you can do with a group? Why?

Lesson 06 / A New Hobby

2. Useful Expressions

Match the expressions (a-d) to its similar meaning (1-4).

A. We're forming a new club.

B. Do you belong to any clubs?

C. What do you do with your down time?

D. I never would've guessed you liked dancing.

1. I didn't know you were into dancing.

2. Are you a part of any organizations?

3. A bunch of us are getting together to start a new hobby.

4. What do you do when you're off work?

3. Key Conversation

Think of the useful expressions and practice the dialogue.

I Didn't Know You Liked Dancing

Amber Kevin, what's that poster you've got there?

Kevin Oh, just a notice for registration for ballroom dancing. We're forming a new club.

Amber Wow, I never would've guessed you liked dancing!

Kevin It's great exercise. Besides, I get to meet lots of great people. What do you do with your down time?

Amber Nothing productive! Just the standard shopping, reading, and hanging out with friends.

Kevin Any interest? We have a free demo lesson this Friday at 7:00.

Amber Actually, that sounds pretty fun. How did you get involved with dance?

Kevin Truth be told, an old girlfriend dragged me into it, but now it's become a big part of my life.

Amber It looks so complicated. Think a klutz like me has a chance?

Kevin Absolutely! I have two left feet myself!

Questions

1. Do you think Kevin enjoyed dancing at first?

2. Do you think Amber will attend the demo lesson?

3. Would you like to take dance lessons?

4. Do you think dancing is a good activity for couples?

A New Hobby

TOP 5 Types of Clubs

1. Volunteering
2. Sports
3. Religious
4. Academic
5. Music & Art

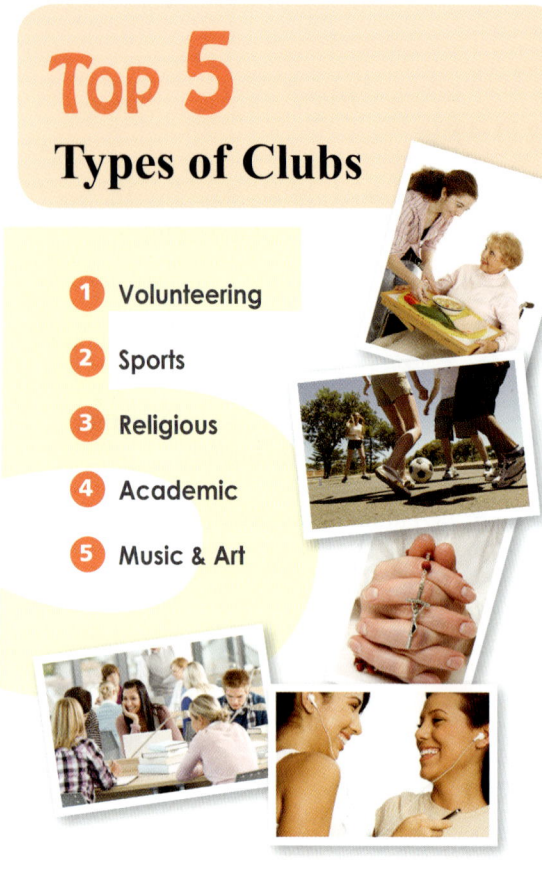

TOP 5 Reasons to Join a Club

1. Create opportunities to meet new people
2. Crystallize your interests and career objectives
3. Network with people in your industry
4. Relieve stress from the workplace
5. Develop my soft skills

Soft skills are personality traits that enable someone to interact effectively with others, like:

- optimism
- responsibility
- integrity
- common sense
- sense of humor

4. Language Practice

Using the key words, complete the sentences then practice making your own sentences.

Practice #1 — First impressions	Practice #2 — Asking about hobbies	Practice #3 — Talking about hobbies
• didn't know / golf • surprised to hear / knitting • never would have guessed / kickboxing ★ _____ you were into _____. ★ I _____ you enjoy _____. ★ I'm _____ you like _____.	• club / these days • activity / spare time • hobby / packed schedule ★ What _____ do you enjoy during your _____? ★ Are you involved with any _____? ★ How do you make time for _____ with your _____?	• collecting coins / I was a kid • ice skating / three years • making jewelry / summer ★ I started _____ this past _____. ★ I've been into _____ since _____. ★ I've been taking _____ lessons for _____.

5. Role Plays

Look at the situations and act out the role plays with your partner.

Situation #1

Role A
You want to invite your friend to an upcoming event with your hiking club.

1. Ask what your friend is doing this Saturday.
2. Invite your friend to go hiking with you and your club.
3. Say that you understand. Agree to do something else with your friend.

Role B
Your friend is inviting you to participate in an event hosted by his or her hiking club. You have severe allergies and try to avoid being outside this time of year.

1. Say that you don't have any plans.
2. Explain why you don't want to go hiking.
3. Invite your friend to join you in another activity.

Role A
You just found out that your coworker enjoys golf. Share an interesting magazine article that you read about golf and invite your coworker to join you on the golf course one day.

1. Explain that you heard that your coworker likes golf.
2. Offer the magazine article you have.
3. Ask if he or she is interested in golfing with you some weekend.

Role B
You are really interested in golf. Engage in a conversation about the topic with your coworker.

1. Confirm that you enjoy golf.
2. Thank your coworker for the article.
3. Accept your coworker's invitation.

Situation #2

Situational Collocations!

Look at the collocations and try making your own sentences.

refined tastes	For a man of humble origin, your husband certainly has refined tastes.
compose poem	Inspired by the moon, he composed a poem.
take comfort from	When I felt lonely I used to take comfort from music.
spend free time	I enjoy spending my free time building Gundam models.
without hesitation	Without hesitation, I'd choose to go fishing when I have time.
abstract painting	I'm into drawing abstract painting these days.
arts and crafts	I made picture frames in the arts and crafts class.
try out	Do you want to try out the new screen-golf center near the park?

1.
2.

A New Hobby

The Best Club for Your Personality Type

Think about your personality characteristics and discuss what clubs you would be most interested in joining.

Outgoing
- friendly
- sociable
- extroverted
- always confident
- open with one's emotions

Sports Club
Dance Club
Hiking Club
Cycling Club
Volunteering Club
Charity Club
Movie Club
Fan Club
Study Club
Wine Club
Book Club
Knitting Club
Meditation Club

- mostly quiet
- dislikes sharing one's emotions
- more restrained

Reserved

6. Cultural Discussion Questions

Talk about the questions in as much detail as possible.

1. What do you think are the most popular hobbies for people in your age group?

2. Are there any hobbies that are typically considered men's or women's hobbies in your country? Why do you think that is?

3. Some people prefer to spend a lot of money on top-of-the-line equipment as soon as they take up a new hobby while others prefer to start with cheap equipment and upgrade when they are sure they are serious about their new hobby. How about you?

4. In your country, what are some popular recreational activities to do in the current season? Explain.

Did You Know?

Read and discuss how you feel about each fact.

1. Did you know that the most popular recreational sport activity in the US is **bowling**?

2. Did you know that the most popular leisure activities in the USA are **reading, watching TV,** and spending time with **family and friends**?

CHOOSE AN EPIC NAME!

If you are creating a club, be sure to give it an interesting, fun name that will help to attract members. You may also want to consider whether it is possible to abbreviate your name so that it sounds great when shortened.

P.L.A.N.T. might stand for **P**eople [who] **L**ike **A**nimals, **N**ature, and **T**rees.

S.T.E.P.S. is the name of an eco-friendly club which was established to accomplish the goal of "GOING GREEN." It stands for **S**teps **T**owards **E**nvironmental **P**rotection **S**ervices.

Q Tell about your favorite club that you have participated in. What was it called? What did you do?

7. Slang & Idioms

Match the slang phrases and idioms with their definitions and use them to complete the sentences below.

1. ___ taken up
2. ___ make a little money on the side
3. ___ throw in the towel
4. ___ if money were no object
5. ___ pay my dues

A. to abandon a struggle
B. if the cost didn't matter
C. to make an official payment to an organization you belong to
D. to become interested or engaged in something
E. to make extra money in addition to one's regular job

1. I told Jennifer she should sell her bracelets to _____.

2. It's time to _____ again at the country club. I feel like I just did it.

3. I've been trying all day to perfect my golf swing, but I think it's time to _____.

4. I've recently _____ knitting. It's a great way to relax at the end of the day.

5. _____, what hobby would you take up?

Wrapping Up!
Write down four things you learned from this lesson and review.

1. _____
2. _____
3. _____
4. _____

07 What Do You Recommend?

» **Learning Objective**

Upon completion of this lesson, you will be able to...

make recommendations to other people when ordering from a menu.

» **Expression Check**

- ☑ I highly recommend getting the steak.
- ☑ You should try the roast chicken. It's so good.
- ☑ I'd definitely order that if I were you.

1. Warm Up Activity

Describe what is happening in the picture.

Talk about the questions.

1. Do you usually follow your friends' and family's recommendations when dining out, or do you prefer to order on your own?

2. What happened the last time you listened to someone's recommendation?

3. In your opinion, is it helpful to ask the restaurant staff for a recommendation? Why or why not?

2. Useful Expressions

Match the expressions (a-d) to its similar meaning (1-4).

A I highly recommend it. ★   ★ 1 That dish is really awful.

B That really hit the spot last time. ★   ★ 2 That was so good when I ate here before.

C Don't even think about trying that. ★   ★ 3 I rate it quite highly.

D I give it five stars. ★   ★ 4 I really think you should try it.

3. Key Conversation

🎧 **Think of the useful expressions and practice the dialogue.**

"What Should I Order?"

Trisha What are you going to get, Grandma?

Edith I don't know. I've heard their meatloaf is great, but I've never been here for lunch before.

Trisha Really? You make great meatloaf at home. Why don't you try something different? Like the Cajun Chicken Salad. Here, take a look. I usually get my dressing on the side.

Edith This one here? I don't think so. The last time I ordered Cajun food, it was way too spicy for me.

Trisha Well, how about the lasagna? Kelly said she gave it five stars.

Edith That sounds good, but it might be a little heavy for lunch.

Trisha Well, I liked the Italian sub I had here last time. Here, look, you can get fries, potato chips, veggies, or beans for your side dish.

Edith All right. As long as they don't slip any onions in it.

Trisha Trust me—you'll love it!

Questions

1. Do you think Edith is a picky eater?
2. Do you think Edith wants her granddaughter's advice?
3. What do you think Edith will do if she does not like her food?
4. Would you rather order something familiar or try something new when eating out?

What Do You Recommend?

The Top 3 Highest Rated Street Foods

① Cheese Steaks in Philadelphia, USA

It is a sandwich made from thinly-sliced pieces of steak and melted cheese in a long roll. A popular regional fast food, it has its roots in the city of Philadelphia, Pennsylvania, USA.

"average $7~$11"

② Cornish Pastry in London, England

It is a pastry filled with sliced beef, diced potato, turnips, and onion, seasoned with salt and pepper, and then baked.

"average £3.40 ($4.30)"

③ Crepes in Paris, France

It is a type of very thin pancake that is served with a variety of fillings.

"average $7.97"

Q1. What is the most popular street food in your country?
Q2. When might people prefer eating street food to going to a sit-down restaurant? Explain.

4. Language Practice

Using the key words, complete the sentences then practice making your own sentences.

Practice #1 — Giving a recommendation

- go for
- recommend
- give / a try

★ I'd like to _____ the spinach calzone.

★ You should _____ the nachos _____.

★ I'd _____ the Buffalo wings if I were you.

Practice #2 — Giving an ordering tip

- stay away from / shrimp
- get the dressing on the side
- substitute steamed veggies

★ If you're ordering the Caesar salad, you might want to _____.

★ You ought to see if they'll _____ for the fries.

★ You should _____ the _____ here.

Practice #3 — Ask for recommendations

- recommend here
- suggest / order
- get today

★ What do you _____ I _____?

★ Is there anything that you _____?

★ What do you think I should _____?

5. Role Plays

Look at the situations and act out the role plays with your partner.

Situation #1

Role A

You have taken your coworker to your favorite restaurant. You know the menu very well. Recommend an item for your coworker to try and talk about the dish.

1. Tell your coworker about the food that the restaurant serves.
2. Ask questions about his or her food preferences.
3. Recommend something for your coworker to order.

Role B

Your coworker has taken you to his or her favorite restaurant. Let your coworker recommend a dish for you to try. Make sure to tell your coworker if you have any allergies or special dietary needs.

1. Ask your coworker for a recommendation.
2. Tell your coworker what kind of food you usually enjoy.
3. Thank your coworker for the recommendation.

Situation #2

Role A

You are a server at a restaurant. Your restaurant does not have an English menu. You have a foreign customer who cannot read the menu. Ask questions to recommend an item from the menu.

1. Ask the customer if he or she needs help.
2. Ask questions to determine what food to recommend to the customer.
3. Describe the dish that you are recommending.

Role B

You are a tourist visiting a foreign country. You stopped in a local restaurant for lunch and found out they do not offer an English menu. Talk to the server to find something that you would like to order.

1. Explain that you cannot read the menu.
2. Tell the server what kind of meat and flavors that you enjoy.
3. Accept the recommendation and order that food.

Situational Collocations!

Look at the collocations and try making your own sentences.

rich taste	The rich taste of chocolate was something we had never tasted.
proper nutrition	Proper nutrition is essential to maintain your health.
fatty food	I am trying to keep off fatty food.
dark meat	Would you like white or dark meat for your chicken patty?
give a try	I'm going to give this a try!
sugar-free	Do you have any sugar-free desserts?
soft serve	Which type of ice cream do you prefer, soft serve or popsicles?
house specialty	What's the house specialty today?

1. ....
2. ....

What Do You Recommend?

FUN PASTA SHAPES

❶ Macaroni
Versatile and goes well for a variety of dishes. Often mixed with meaty sauces and cheese

❷ Penne
Served best with meat, fish, or hearty vegetable mixes. Can be fried or baked.

❸ Spaghetti
Served with tomato based sauces, fish, and shellfish

❹ Bow Ties (Farfalle)
Mixes well with all sauces and cold pasta salads

❺ Lasagna
Served layered with tomato sauce and meat then baked

❻ Fusilli or Rotini
Spiral shape helps its hold on to thick sauces and seafood

❼ Angel hair
Best with light sauces, delicate cream, and herbs

❽ Fettuccini or Tagliatelle
Goes well with thick cream sauces and ground beef, vegetables, and cheese

Q1. What other pasta types are you familiar with?

Q2. Which type of pasta do you enjoy the most?

6. Cultural Discussion Questions

Talk about the questions in as much detail as possible.

1. Do you read restaurant reviews when traveling? Are they helpful when deciding what to eat?

2. What is a dish from your country that you would recommend to a foreign visitor? Describe the dish in detail.

3. Are there any restaurants in your city that you would recommend to a tourist? Why?

4. What is one food from your country that you would recommend that visitors avoid trying? Why?

Did You Know?

Read and discuss how you feel about each fact.

1. Did you know that **one-third** of Americans **worked in a restaurant** for their first jobs?

2. Did you know that **millennials** spend **44%** of their **food budget** at restaurants?

Fun Facts About Food

You would have to walk for seven hours straight to burn off a Super Sized Coke, fries, and Big Mac.

The toxic puffer fish delicacy called Fugu kills about 300 people per year. The emperor of Japan can eat Fugu only when it is going to be his last meal.

The largest item on any menu in the world is the roast camel. The camel is stuffed with a sheep's carcass, which is then stuffed with chickens, which are then stuffed with fish, which are finally stuffed with eggs. This is a rare delicacy and is mostly served at Bedouin wedding feasts.

Q1. What is the strangest food you have ever eaten? Did you enjoy it?

Q2. Have you ever eaten anything that made you sick? What was it?

7. Slang & Idioms

Match the slang phrases and idioms with their definitions and use them to complete the sentences below.

1. ___ hit the spot   A. to have consumed food in such a large quantity that you feel very full

2. ___ foodie   B. a person who is selective about what he or she eats

3. ___ totally stuffed   C. ordinary but fundamental things; basic ingredients

4. ___ picky eater   D. to be exactly what is required

5. ___ meat-and-potatoes   E. a person who loves food and is very interested in different types of food

1. I'm a _____ kind of guy – I like the basics and none of that fancy fusion stuff.

2. Melissa is a _____. She drives for miles just to try out popular dishes.

3. Their mozzarella sticks really _____.

4. My son is such a _____. It's really hard to find anything he wants to order.

5. I'm _____! Thanks for your recommendation.

Wrapping Up!

Write down four things you learned from this lesson and review.

1. _____
2. _____
3. _____
4. _____

Back to Work

08 Back to **Work**

» **Learning Objective**

Upon completion of this lesson, you will be able to...

talk about your past weekend in detail.

» **Expression Check**

- ☑ What did you do over the weekend?
- ☑ I didn't get up to too much.
- ☑ I was basically a couch potato all weekend.

1. Warm Up Activity

Describe what is happening in the picture.

> Talk about the questions.

1. What is your busiest day of the week?
2. What do you usually do on the weekend?
2. What would you do if you had a long weekend?

2. Useful Expressions

Match the expressions (a-d) to its similar meaning (1-4).

A Did you have a nice weekend?

B What was your weekend like?

C What did you get up to over the weekend?

D I was basically a couch potato all weekend.

1 Was your weekend good?

2 Did you do anything exciting over the weekend?

3 I spent the weekend on the sofa.

4 What were your days off like?

3. Key Conversation

Think of the useful expressions and practice the dialogue.

There's Nothing Like It!

Lisa Hey, Raj!

Raj Oh, hi Lisa.

Lisa How was your weekend?

Raj I didn't get up to too much. How about you?

Lisa The same. I was basically a couch potato all weekend.

Raj Really? I thought your sister was in town.

Lisa Yeah, but we just hung out at home. She's kind of a homebody.

Raj Ah, I see. Kind of like me, then.

Lisa Really?

Raj Sure! There's nothing like spending a day at home with a warm cup of tea and a good movie.

Lisa Maybe I should introduce you guys.

Raj Keep me posted. I'm game for anything.

Questions

1. Do you think Lisa enjoyed her weekend with her sister?
2. What kind of personality does Lisa's sister have?
3. Do you think Raj likes spending time alone or with other people?
4. Do you think Raj will like Lisa's sister?

Back to Work

How to Beat the Monday Blues

Here are some tips to make Monday mornings a little easier.

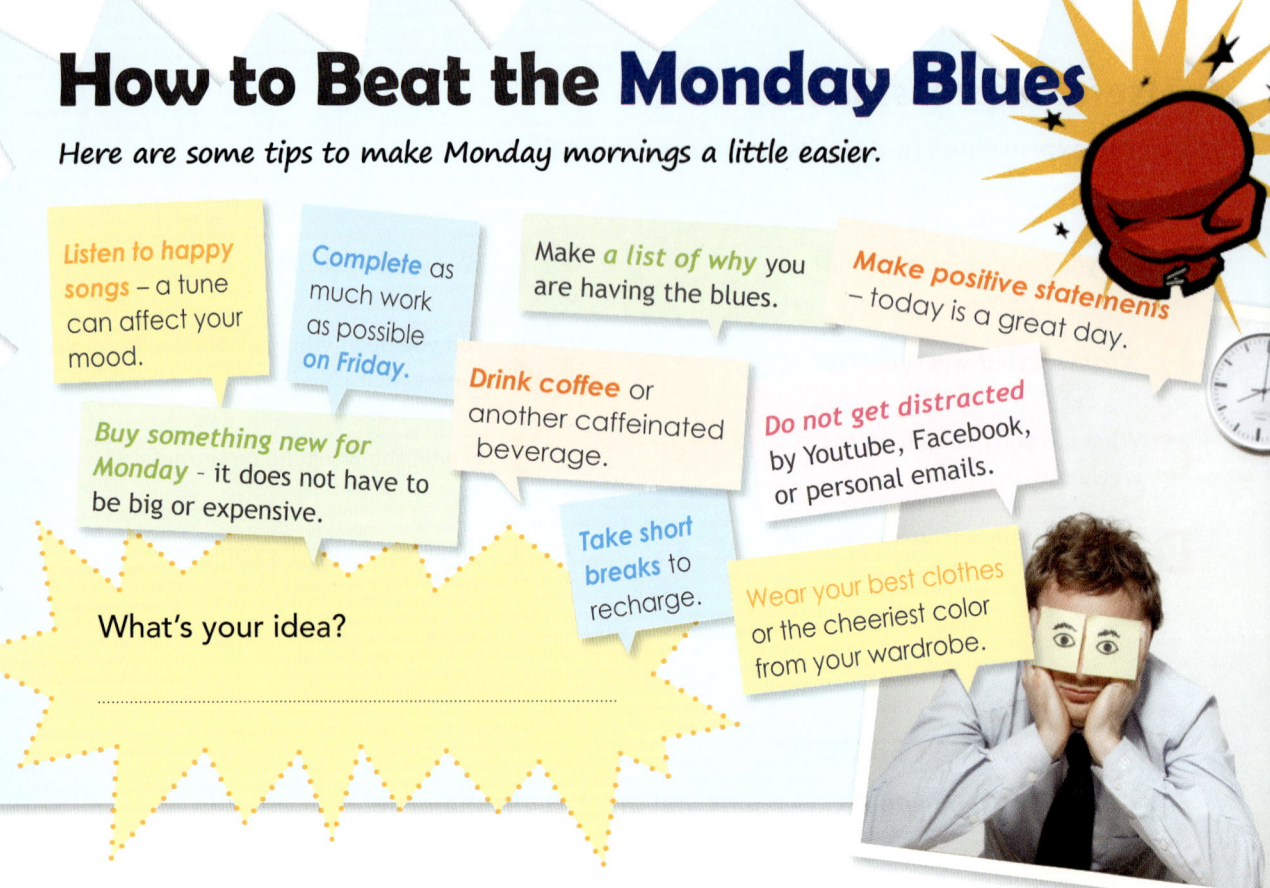

- **Listen to happy songs** – a tune can affect your mood.
- **Complete** as much work as possible **on Friday**.
- Make **a list of why** you are having the blues.
- **Make positive statements** – today is a great day.
- **Buy something new for Monday** - it does not have to be big or expensive.
- **Drink coffee** or another caffeinated beverage.
- **Do not get distracted** by Youtube, Facebook, or personal emails.
- **Take short breaks** to recharge.
- **Wear your best clothes** or the cheeriest color from your wardrobe.

What's your idea?
....

4. Language Practice

Using the key words, complete the sentences then practice making your own sentences.

Practice #1 — Follow-up questions

- What did you see?
- What movie did you watch?
- Why did you have to work?

★ A: I had to work over the weekend.
 B: _____?

★ A: I went to a concert on Saturday night.
 B: _____?

★ A: I went to the movies this weekend.
 B: _____?

Practice #2 — Activities

- went for a hike / Saturday
- deep cleaned my apartment /weekend
- played soccer / Sunday afternoon

★ I _____ _____ all _____.

★ I _____ with my friends on _____.

★ I _____ in the mountains on _____.

Practice #3 — How about you?

- had a few beers / last Saturday
- attended church / Sunday morning
- worked on the project report /over the weekend

★ I _____ on _____.

★ I _____ _____ at the office _____.

★ We _____ at the party _____.

5. Role Plays

Look at the situations and act out the role plays with your partner.

Situation #1

Role A
You and your neighbor are good friends. You see your neighbor in the hall after a 4-day weekend. Ask what your neighbor did over the long weekend.

1. Greet your neighbor and ask about his or her weekend.
2. Ask about what your neighbor did.
3. Tell your neighbor you just stayed home and relaxed.

Role B
You and your neighbor are close. You just came back from an amazing trip to Guam. Tell your neighbor about your weekend.

1. Tell your neighbor where you went.
2. Talk about the activities you did.
3. Ask your neighbor about his or her weekend.

Situation #2

Role A
It's Monday morning and you are back at work. Make small talk to your coworker about what you did last weekend. You stayed at home and cleaned your house.

1. Ask your coworker what he or she did last weekend.
2. Say that your coworker's weekend sounds exciting.
3. Explain what you did.

Role B
Talk to your coworker about what you did last weekend. You went to a concert with some of your friends.

1. Tell your coworker what you did.
2. Ask about your coworker's weekend.
3. Invite your coworker to join you next time.

Situational Collocations!

Look at the collocations and try making your own sentences.

flew by	I can't believe it's Monday. The weekend flew by so fast.
chill out	We sometimes meet up to chill out and watch a movie.
caught up on	I caught up on movies last weekend.
get-together	Didn't you say that you have a family get-together?
make it	My older sister said she couldn't make it to our trip.
family reunion	I saw dozens of my relatives at the annual family reunion.
weekend off	The kids went to summer camp, so we got the weekend off!
suffer from hangover	I spent my whole weekend suffering from hangover.

1.
2.

Feeling Blue?

The word blue is used to express both negative and positive meanings. Look at the following expressions and guess which ones have positive or negative meanings.

Out of the blue: unexpected

True blue: someone loyal and faithful

Baby blue: very light blue; a person's blue eyes

Feeling blue: feeling sad or depressed

The Blues: a popular style of music sometimes characterized by melancholy melodies and words

Singing the blues: moaning about one's circumstances

6. Cultural Discussion Questions

Talk about the questions in as much detail as possible.

1. How do most people in your country spend their weekends?
2. Do you prefer to spend your weekend relaxing, or do you try to keep busy? Explain.
3. What would life be like without weekends? What if weekends were three days instead of two?
4. Do you believe in working on the weekend?

Did You Know?

Read and discuss how you feel about each fact.

1. Did you know that in many Islamic countries the weekend is either **Thursday and Friday** or **Friday and Saturday**?
2. Did you know that the average Canadian has **4 hours** of leisure time on weekdays and **7.5 hours** on weekend days?

Lesson 08 / Back to Work 57

The Happiest Day of the Week

In a survey, participants were asked what they thought their mood was for each day of the week.

65% believed their worst moods were on **Monday mornings.**

35% believed their worst moods were on **Monday evenings.**

43% believed their best moods were on **Friday evenings.**

45% believed their best moods were on **Saturday mornings.**

When are your best and worst days of the week? Use the descriptions below to help explain your mood on each day.

- ☐ Happy
- ☐ Awake
- ☐ Energetic
- ☐ Calm
- ☐ Relaxed
- ☐ Melancholy
- ☐ Moody

- ☐ Cheerful
- ☐ Content
- ☐ Depressed
- ☐ Drained
- ☐ Blank
- ☐ Sad
- ☐ Sleepy

- ☐ Excited
- ☐ Exhausted
- ☐ Gloomy
- ☐ Anxious
- ☐ Thankful
- ☐ Peaceful
- ☐ Nervous

7. Slang & Idioms

Match the slang phrases and idioms with their definitions and use them to complete the sentences below.

1. ___ TGIF
2. ___ catch up on lost sleep
3. ___ went out for brunch
4. ___ take it easy
5. ___ running errands

A. to make up sleep that you missed earlier
B. to go out to buy or do something
C. to relax and rest
D. to eat a late morning meal
E. an acronym for "Thank God It's Friday"

1. I didn't do much besides _____.
2. This weekend, I'm going to _____. I've been working hard all week.
3. I can't believe this week is finally over! _____!
4. I spent most of Saturday _____.
5. On Sunday, we slept in and _____.

Wrapping Up!

Write down four things you learned from this lesson and review.

I Need to Cancel

09 I Need to Cancel

» **Learning Objective**

Upon completion of this lesson, you will be able to...

cancel a plan that you have made with someone.

» **Expression Check**

☑ I'm really sorry, but I have to cancel our appointment.
☑ It's no problem. Do you want to reschedule?
☑ Unfortunately, something came up, and I have to cancel.

1. Warm Up Activity

Describe what is happening in the picture.

Talk about the questions.

1. Have you ever had to cancel an appointment at the last minute?
2. What are some reasons that you might need to cancel an appointment?
3. What would you do if you forgot an appointment?

2. Useful Expressions

Match the expressions (a-d) to its similar meaning (1-4).

A Something came up.

B Do you want to reschedule?

C Sorry, I'm running late.

D You need to give 24-hours' notice to cancel.

1 Do you want to get together another time?

2 I'm late for our meeting.

3 You need to cancel at least 24 hours before the appointment.

4 Something happened, and I won't be able to make it.

3. Key Conversation

Think of the useful expressions and practice the dialogue.

It's No Problem

Jeremy	Hi Michelle. Could I talk to you for a minute?
Michelle	Sure, Jeremy. What's up?
Jeremy	I'm really sorry, but I have to cancel our appointment.
Michelle	It's no problem. Do you want to reschedule?
Jeremy	Please, if you don't mind.
Michelle	How does next Monday at 2:30 sound?
Jeremy	Is it possible to meet earlier than that?
Michelle	Well, I have a few minutes before lunch, maybe at around 11:30?
Jeremy	Hm. I think I'd better stick with 2:30 then.
Michelle	Alright. I'll see you on Monday then.

Questions

1. What do you think their relationship is?
2. When will Jeremy and Michelle meet?
3. Why do you think Jeremy prefers the 2:30 meeting over the 11:30 meeting?
4. Do you think that Michelle is disappointed about not meeting Jeremy today?

I Need to Cancel

Cultural Schedule Difficulties

Next Friday? vs. This Friday?

If today is Monday, December 28th, and I refer to "this Friday", most people will understand Friday, January 1st. The trouble is that not everyone would use the words "this Friday." Some people would refer to Friday, January 1st, as "next Friday."

01/12/2015 vs. 12/01/2015

You need to pay attention when writing numerical dates. If you have an international audience, it is much wiser to spell out the relevant month. Instead of writing either 01/12/2015 or 12/01/2015, use either 12 January 2015 or January 12, 2015.

Most online forms have now solved this problem. The confusion today is related to people not being aware of their global audience.

4. Language Practice

Using the key words, complete the sentences then practice making your own sentences.

Practice #1 — Canceling

- came up / make it to
- cancel / appointment
- rescheduling / meeting

★ I have to _____ our _____.

★ Would you mind _____ our _____?

★ Something _____ at the last minute and I can't _____ dinner.

Practice #2 — Rescheduling

- give 24 hours' notice / cancel the appointment
- meeting / pushed back
- no problem / reschedule

★ They require that you _____ to _____.

★ It's _____! Let's _____ to next week.

★ Did you hear that our _____ was _____?

Practice #3 — Giving reasons

- running late / go ahead
- come up / need to cancel
- take a rain check / do it another day

★ I'm going to need to _____ _____. Could we _____?

★ Sorry, but something's _____. I _____.

★ I'm _____. _____ without me.

5. Role Plays

Look at the situations and act out the role plays with your partner.

Situation #1

Role A

You scheduled a dentist appointment for this afternoon at 2:00 p.m., but you need to cancel because you have too much urgent work to get done. Call the clinic and speak with the receptionist to reschedule.

1. Explain the situation.
2. Ask to reschedule to next week.
3. Ask if you can make an appointment at the same time next Tuesday.

Role B

You are the receptionist at a busy dental clinic. Help a patient reschedule his or her appointment to next week.

1. Confirm the patient's name and original appointment time.
2. Ask which day the patient can come in.
3. Confirm the details of the new appointment before ending the call.

Situation #2

Role A

You have not seen one of your closest friends in almost two months. You planned to have dinner together this weekend and you are looking forward to catching up with your friend.

1. Answer the phone and ask how your friend has been.
2. Accept your friend's apology.
3. Offer to reschedule the appointment to next weekend.

Role B

You are supposed to have dinner with a close friend on Saturday. You haven't seen each other in two months. You are very excited about the plan but found out that you need to attend a family event in a different city. Call and explain the situation and reschedule the dinner.

1. Apologize to your friend and cancel the appointment.
2. Give a reason for canceling.
3. Arrange a time to meet next weekend.

Situational Collocations!

Look at the collocations and try making your own sentences.

another time	Sorry about missing out, I'll make it up to you another time.
work late	I can't make it tonight. I need to work late.
little difficult	It's a little difficult to leave the house right now.
possibly reschedule	Could you possibly reschedule us for tomorrow?
inconvenience caused	To our customer, we apologize for the inconvenience caused by the delays.
make it	I don't think I can make it then, I work night-shift.
later time	Could we move that to a later time?
free time	When is your next free time?

1. ....

2. ....

I Need to Cancel

Time-related Expressions

Time is precious. Most of us do not have enough of it and wish we had more. There are lots of English expressions using time. Here are some expressions.

in the nick of time — You arrive or finish something at the last possible moment, just before it is too late.

out of time — There is no more time left to do something. The time limit or deadline has been reached.

make time — Finding the time to do something. We have to clear some time in our schedules to do something.

kill time — To do something that is not very interesting or important to pass time. Usually we do this when we are waiting for something that will take place later.

6. Cultural Discussion Questions

Talk about the questions in as much detail as possible.

1. If you are late, what message does it give to the person who is waiting for you?
2. In your culture, is it better to arrive early, on time, or a little bit late for a meeting?
3. Is it rude to cancel an appointment in your culture? What is the best way to do it without offending the person you made plans with?
4. Which of these appointments is the easiest to cancel: a doctor's appointment, business meeting for work, or an outing with friends? Which is the hardest?

Did You Know?

Read and discuss how you feel about each fact.

1. Did you know **missed doctor's appointments** cost the U.S. healthcare system **$150 billion** in lost revenue per year?
2. Did you know a recent survey of **2,000** Americans aged 18 to 54 revealed that 80 percent of us **lie** or make excuses to **avoid going out**?

Which One Should I Cancel?!

Have you ever accidentally scheduled two appointments at the same time and needed to cancel one? Most people have had this experience. To decide which appointment to cancel or reschedule, it is important to think about the benefits and costs of canceling each appointment.

Imagine that you made plans to have lunch with a co-worker in 10 minutes and your boss suddenly requests a meeting to deal with a pressing problem. Of course, you would cancel your lunch plans because of the urgency of the meeting with your boss.

Read through the time management matrix on the right. It will help you take control of your schedule by guiding you to prioritize meetings according to importance and urgency.

HIGH IMPORTANCE

I. Urgent and Important
- Your child had an accident
- Your boss requests an urgent meeting

II. Important but Not Urgent:
- Doing daily household chores
- Spending quality time with children/family

HIGH URGENCY

III. Urgent but Not Important
- Shopping for groceries
- Receiving some phone calls
- Checking emails

IV. Not Urgent and Not Important
- Surfing the Internet aimlessly
- Watching a soap opera on TV

Time Management Matrix

7. Slang & Idioms

Match the slang phrases and idioms with their definitions and use them to complete the sentences below.

1. ___ running behind schedule
2. ___ something came up
3. ___ push back
4. ___ double-booked
5. ___ break the news

A. something unexpected happened
B. to have scheduled two things at a conflicting time
C. tell someone something they did not expect or bad news
D. to do something later than planned
E. to delay

1. I hate to _____, but I can't make it to the get together.
2. Could we _____ our meeting to next week?
3. Sorry, but I'm _____. You guys should just go without me.
4. I'm sorry to cancel, but _____.
5. Sorry, but I've accidentally _____ myself.

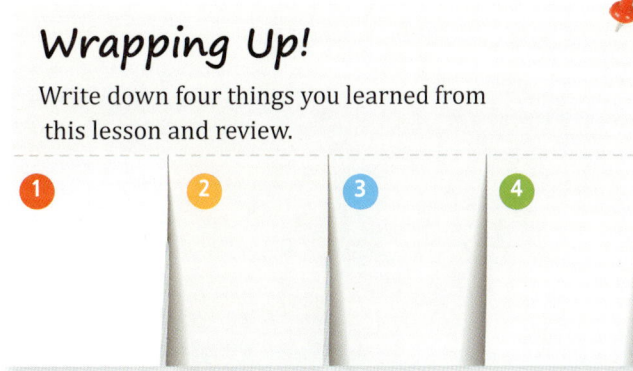

Wrapping Up!
Write down four things you learned from this lesson and review.

1
2
3
4

Monthly Bills

10

Monthly Bills

» Learning Objective

Upon completion of this lesson, you will be able to...

discuss paying monthly bills.

» Expression Check

- ☑ I'd like to pay my monthly utility bill, please.
- ☑ Can I pay my cell phone bill here as well?
- ☑ That should make us even.

1. Warm Up Activity

Describe what is happening in the picture.

Talk about the questions.

1. What bills do you have to pay each month?
2. How do you usually pay your bills?
3. Have you ever missed a payment deadline? What happened?

2. Useful Expressions

Match the expressions (a-d) to its similar meaning (1-4).

A I'd like to pay my monthly utility bill, please.

B That should square us up.

C Our rent is increasing again.

D How much is your cell phone plan?

1 The cost to live here is going up again.

2 I need to pay for the services I use every month.

3 How much do you pay each month to use your cell phone?

4 That should make us even.

3. Key Conversation

Think of the useful expressions and practice the dialogue.

Forgot to Pay the Bills

Cashier	Hi, welcome to Kor-Tel. What can I do for you today?
Ian	Yes, I was wondering how I can get my TV and Internet working again.
Cashier	Sure. What seems to be the problem?
Ian	Well, they got shut off while I was on vacation. I guess I forgot to pay the bills.
Cashier	Yeah, that would do it. Would you like to pay the bill today?
Ian	I may as well, and could I pay my cell phone bill here, too?
Cashier	Sure, no problem. What is the number on your account?
Ian	347-555-7294.
Cashier	OK. It looks like you owe $157.68.
Ian	Okay. I'd like to put it on my card.
Cashier	Great. Your cable and Internet should be back on within the next 30 minutes.
Ian	Thank you very much.

Questions

1. Do you think Ian took a long vacation? Why?
2. Where do you think he is paying the bill?
3. Do you think his cable and Internet costs are expensive?
4. Do you think Ian will forget to pay his bills again?

Monthly Bills

Paying Monthly Bills

Which items do you pay a monthly bill for? How much do you usually pay?

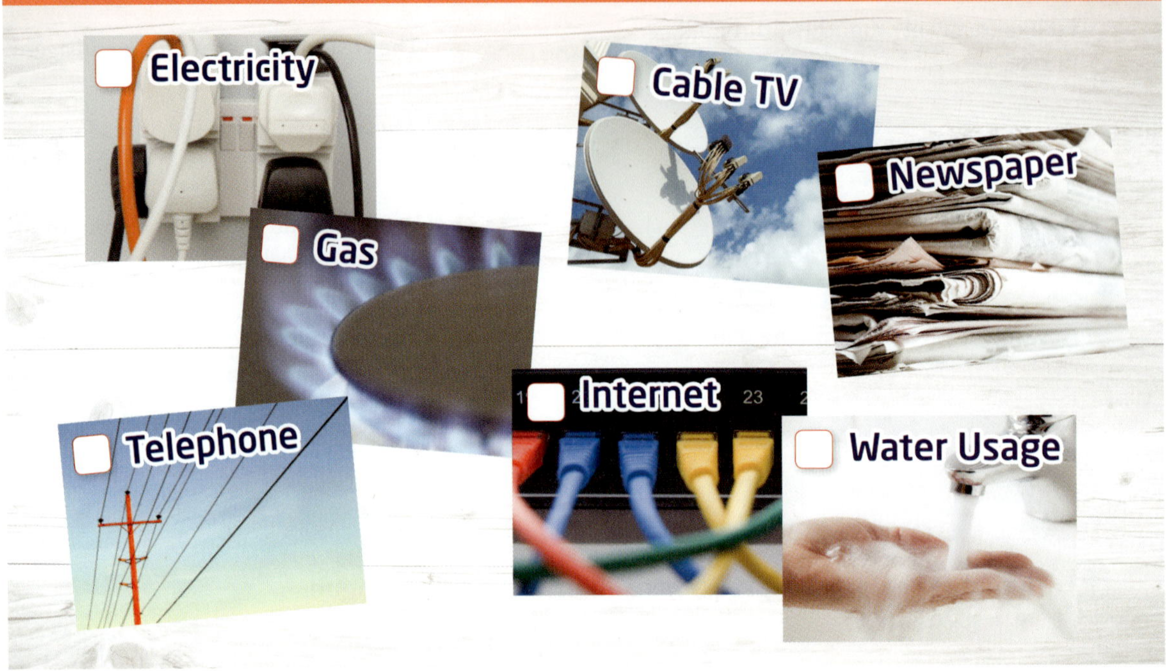

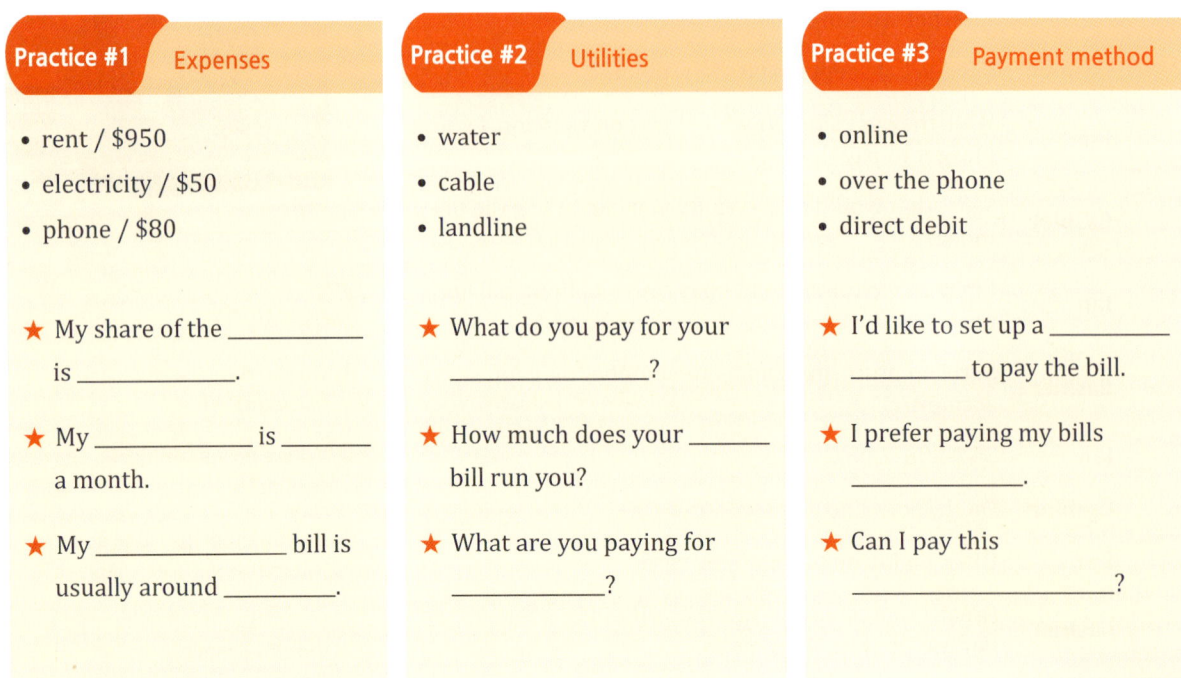

- ☐ Electricity
- ☐ Cable TV
- ☐ Newspaper
- ☐ Gas
- ☐ Internet
- ☐ Telephone
- ☐ Water Usage

4. Language Practice

Using the key words, complete the sentences then practice making your own sentences.

Practice #1 — Expenses

- rent / $950
- electricity / $50
- phone / $80

★ My share of the _____ is _____.

★ My _____ is _____ a month.

★ My _____ bill is usually around _____.

Practice #2 — Utilities

- water
- cable
- landline

★ What do you pay for your _____?

★ How much does your _____ bill run you?

★ What are you paying for _____?

Practice #3 — Payment method

- online
- over the phone
- direct debit

★ I'd like to set up a _____ _____ to pay the bill.

★ I prefer paying my bills _____.

★ Can I pay this _____?

Lesson 10 / Monthly Bills **67**

5. Role Plays

Look at the situations and act out the role plays with your partner.

Situation #1

Role A

You are the landlord of an apartment building. One of your tenants is two weeks late with his or her rent. Visit in person to discuss the problem.

1. Explain why you are visiting.
2. Tell the tenant that this cannot happen again.
3. Discuss how the tenant will pay for this month's rent.

Role B

Your landlord just knocked on your door. You realize now that you forgot to pay your rent this month. Offer to correct the problem right away.

1. Apologize for the situation.
2. Explain that you have been busy with work and you simply forgot.
3. Offer to pay by bank transfer right now.

Situation #2

Role A

You are a customer who wants to pay your cell phone bill at the store. Ask an employee for help.

1. Ask if you can pay the bill in the store.
2. Put the bill on your credit card.
3. Agree to set up a direct debit for next month's bill.

Role B

You are an employee at a telecom company. A customer needs help paying his or her bill in the store. Help the customer and explain the benefits of setting up a direct debit to pay the bill directly from his or her bank account.

1. Tell the customer that you accept payments by credit card.
2. Tell the customer about how setting up a direct debit would save him or her time.
3. Offer to set up a direct debit beginning with next month's bill.

Situational Collocations!

Look at the collocations and try making your own sentences.

large bill	I got a rather large water bill this month.
cut off	Verizon cut off my internet because I didn't pay my bills.
due date	Are there any advantages for paying bills before the due date?
late fees	I need to pay off the late fees before they stack.
current charge	The current charge for my gas bill is $10.
long distance	All these long distance called racked up this month's phone bills.
water meter	Check your water meter regularly for any leaks.
final notice	The electricity gave me a final notice before cutting of my energy.

1. ....

2. ....

Monthly Bills

How Much?
Charting the Bills

In the space below, draw a pie graph based on the amount you spend on each of your monthly bills.

* Utility bills
  (Electricity, Gas, Water, and Telephone)
* Internet / TV / Newspaper
* Insurance fees
* Rental fee
* Cell phone
* Credit cards

6. Cultural Discussion Questions

Talk about the questions in as much detail as possible.

1. Do you think that the cost of living is too high in your country? Why do you feel that way?
2. How do most people in your country pay their utility bills?
3. Should the poor be exempt from paying taxes or utility bills?
4. Are there any advantages to paying your monthly bills with a credit card? Explain.

Did You Know?

Read and discuss how you feel about each fact.

1. Did you know that **three out of the five** most **expensive cities** to live in worldwide are in **Switzerland**?
2. Did you know the **Solomon Islands** has the highest electricity cost in the world, at a staggering **99 US cents** per kilowatt-hour?

How Often Do You...?

Think about what you do on a regular basis.

1. **Daily** — Read a daily newspaper
2. **Weekly** — Have a weekly meeting
3. **Monthly** — Receive a monthly salary
4. **Quarterly** — Hold a quarterly sales meeting
5. **Yearly** — Have a Christmas party

7. Slang & Idioms

Match the slang phrases and idioms with their definitions and use them to complete the sentences below.

1. ___ go broke
2. ___ pay off
3. ___ skyrocketed
4. ___ living hand to mouth
5. ___ highway robbery

A. to barely make enough to pay one's living expenses
B. to rise extremely quickly
C. excessive profit from a business transaction
D. to no longer have money
E. to pay (a debt or a creditor) in full

1. The amount that the company charges for its service is _____!

2. My electricity bills _____ the past few months because of the hot weather.

3. Karen took a second job to help _____ her student loans.

4. After the economic downturn, we've been _____.

5. I'm going to _____ if I pay all my bills at once.

Wrapping Up!

Write down four things you learned from this lesson and review.

1. _____
2. _____
3. _____
4. _____

11 Going to the Doctor

» Learning Objective

Upon completion of this lesson, you will be able to...

visit a doctor and describe your symptoms.

» Expression Check

- ☑ I don't feel very well today.
- ☑ What are your symptoms?
- ☑ I'll prescribe some medicine for you.

1. Warm Up Activity

Describe what is happening in the picture.

Talk about the questions.

1. Do you have regular physical check-ups?
2. Do you usually make an appointment to see a doctor?
3. Do doctors make "house calls" in your country?

Lesson 11 / Going to the Doctor

2. Useful Expressions

Match the expressions (a-d) to its similar meaning (1-4).

A I'm feeling a little under the weather today.

B She made a quick recovery after taking some medicine.

C The doctor needs to take a blood sample and have it analyzed.

D The bus driver wasn't feeling well and called in sick.

1 The doctor has to draw some blood for tests.

2 The bus driver took the day off sick.

3 I don't feel very well today.

4 After she took her medicine, she felt as good as usual.

3. Key Conversation

🎧 Think of the useful expressions and practice the dialogue.

I Am Not Feeling Up to Par…

Dr. Browne	Hello, Mr. Jones. What brings you here today?
Mr. Jones	I haven't been feeling very well.
Dr. Browne	I see. What exactly are your symptoms?
Mr. Jones	I seem to be short of breath lately. I've been feeling tired for the last three days, and I've got a horrible headache that won't go away.
Dr. Browne	I'll need to check your vital signs. Then I'll draw some blood.
Mr. Jones	How long will that take?
Dr. Browne	Not long.

============ (a few hours later) ============

Dr. Browne	Here are your test results.
Mr. Jones	What's my diagnosis?
Dr. Browne	It's a respiratory infection. I'll write you a prescription and you'll be feeling up to par again soon.
Mr. Jones	So it isn't serious?
Dr. Browne	(with a smile) Don't worry, Mr. Jones. You won't drop dead tomorrow!

Questions

1. What was wrong with Mr. Jones?
2. Do you think Dr. Browne is a good doctor?
3. Do you think Mr. Jones will get well soon?
4. Do you think Mr. Jones has seen Dr. Browne before today?

Going to the Doctor

Highest Paid Physicians

There are nearly 100 unique specialties in the medical profession. Have you ever wondered how much these specialists are being paid? Read which medical specialties pay the highest average salaries in the US below.

TOP 5 (Unit: US$/ Average Annual Amount)

01	02	03	04	05
				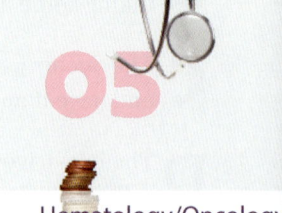
Orthopedic Surgery	Cardiology	Gastroenterology	Urology	Hematology/Oncology
$464,500	$461,364	$441,421	$424,091	$396,000

Q. Do you think specialists deserve higher salaries? Why or why not?

4. Language Practice

Using the key words, complete the sentences then practice making your own sentences.

Practice #1 — Asking about symptoms

- a fever
- your migraine
- the pain in your shoulder

★ Have you taken anything for _____?

★ Have you seen anyone about _____?

★ Did you check if you have _____?

Practice #2 — Treatment

- was hospitalized
- follow this treatment
- undergo surgery

★ If his condition doesn't improve, he'll need to _____.

★ You'll need to _____ for at least ten days.

★ He _____ for observation.

Practice #3 — Finishing up

- write a prescription
- make a diagnosis
- draw blood

★ We'll be able to _____ _____ once the test results come back.

★ The nurse will _____ for the test now.

★ The doctor will _____ _____ for your medication.

5. Role Plays

Look at the situations and act out the role plays with your partner.

Situation #1

Role A
You noticed that one of your co-workers has not been feeling well. Your team is busy with a project now and you are concerned that his or her poor health might slow down the team. Suggest that he or she see a doctor right away.

1. Ask about your co-worker's condition.
2. Suggest that he or she go to a clinic now.
3. Offer to help cover your teammate's work while he or she is gone.

Role B
You have a cold and a sore throat, but your team is too busy with a project for you to go to the doctor.

1. Explain your symptoms.
2. Say that you are too busy.
3. Accept your teammate's offer of help.

Situation #2

Role A
You have been sick for the last couple of weeks. You have a headache and a runny nose. Go and see the doctor to find out what is wrong.

1. Explain your symptoms to the doctor.
2. Tell how long you have been sick.
3. Thank the doctor for seeing you.

Role B
You are a doctor. A sick patient comes to your clinic complaining of classic sinus infection symptoms. Diagnose him or her and write a prescription.

1. Ask the patient about the symptoms.
2. Diagnose the patient.
3. Tell the patient to pick up a prescription from the nurse.

Situational Collocations!

Look at the collocations and try making your own sentences.

visiting hours	I'm sorry, but the visiting hours are over.
stuffy nose	Sounds like you've got a stuffy nose.
sore throat	It's hard to swallow food because of my sore throat.
upset stomach	I think I have upset stomach from dinner.
take pills	Did you take your pills today?
get well soon	I hope you get well soon.
take temperature	I need to take my temperature every few hours.
highly contagious	An outbreak of the highly contagious bird flu is spreading in Korea.

1.
2.

Going to the Doctor

Mom, I Have a Fever...

A normal body temperature is 36°C to 37°C. Fever is a raised body temperature of over 38.5°C. If you have a fever, your body temperature will be higher than normal and you will sweat.

Children often have a high temperature (fever) when they are sick. Most fevers occur to help the body fight an infection. If your child is sick, you may want to use a thermometer to find out if they have a high temperature.

Types of thermometers:
- mercury thermometers – placed under the armpit for 3 minutes
- digital thermometers – placed under the armpit or tongue
- ear thermometers – placed in the ear with a probe tip

Useful Expression "Run a fever / temperature"

To have a higher than normal body temperature

Examples
- "The girl has been running a fever this week."
- "The little boy is running a temperature and should stay in bed all day."

6. Cultural Discussion Questions

Talk about the questions in as much detail as possible.

1. How much does it usually cost to see a doctor in your country? Do you feel like it is too expensive?

2. Do people in your country usually visit the same family doctor every time or do they go directly to a specialist? Explain.

3. What symptoms do you think most people see a doctor about?

4. Tell about the last time you were sick. What treatment did you receive?

Did You Know?

Read and discuss how you feel about each fact.

1. Did you know that studies have found that *optimism is good for your overall health*? It is linked to a healthy heart and avoiding sickness.

2. Did you know that *wearing headphones* for just one hour will increase the bacteria in your ear by *700 times*?

Lesson 11 / Going to the Doctor

Cold vs. Flu

A **cold** usually comes on gradually — over the course of a day or two. Generally, it leaves you feeling tired, sneezing, coughing, and plagued by a running nose.

Flu, on the other hand, comes on suddenly and hits hard. You will feel weak and tired, and you could run a fever as high as 40°C. Your muscles and joints will probably ache, and you will feel chilled and could have a severe headache and sore throat.

Good to Know Expressions

- **get a checkup** : I go to the doctor every year to get a checkup.
- **in the best of health** : My father has been in the best of health for many years.
- **just what the doctor ordered** : A nice hot bath was just what the doctor ordered after my long day at work.
- **run some tests** : The doctor decided to run some tests on the patient.
- **take (someone's) pulse** : The doctor took the patient's pulse when she arrived at the hospital.
- **on crutches** : I fell off my bike and broke my leg. I'm going to be on crutches all summer.
- **in a cast** : He broke his leg a month ago, and his leg is still in a cast.

7. Slang & Idioms

Match the slang phrases and idioms with their definitions and use them to complete the sentences below.

1. ___ sick in bed   A. to appear very healthy
2. ___ green around the gills B. to undergo surgery
3. ___ on the mend   C. remaining in bed while one is ill
4. ___ picture of health   D. improving in health or condition; recovering
5. ___ went under the knife   E. sickly-looking

1. The woman _____ at the hospital last evening.
2. My grandfather is _____ after he broke his leg last week.
3. The man is feeling very well and is the _____.
4. I spent most of the day _____.
5. My colleague was looking a little _____ today.

Wrapping Up!
Write down four things you learned from this lesson and review.

1 2 3 4

The Highlight of My Trip

12

The Highlight of My Trip

» Learning Objective

Upon completion of this lesson, you will be able to...

to discuss places you have traveled with others.

» Expression Check

- ☑ Catch me up on your trip!
- ☑ The highlight for me had to be seeing the Northern Lights.
- ☑ I'll remember it forever.

1. Warm Up Activity

Describe what is happening in the picture.

Talk about the questions.

1. What vacation destinations are most popular among people in your country?
2. Do you prefer to travel domestically or internationally? Why?
3. What is your favorite place you have visited in the world?

2. Useful Expressions

Match the expressions (a-d) to its similar meaning (1-4).

A. What was the highlight of your vacation?

B. Catch me up on your trip!

C. I'll remember it forever.

D. I have so many things to tell you about!

1. What was your favorite moment when you were traveling?

2. It was an unforgettable experience

3. I'm so excited to tell you about my trip.

4. Tell me all about your vacation.

3. Key Conversation

Think of the useful expressions and practice the dialogue.

How Was Your Trip

Kelly	Hi, John! How was your week off?
John	I didn't get up to too much. I ended up just hanging out at home and catching up on my sleep. How was your trip?
Kelly	It was great, thanks! My family had the best time in Hawaii.
John	You look so tan! Did you just relax on the beach the whole time?
Kelly	We did a bit, but we also rented a car and took a lot of day trips.
John	That sounds amazing! What did you see?
Kelly	Well, the highlight of my trip had to be driving the Road to Hana. It's a coastal highway with some amazing views. There were so many interesting places to stop along the way.
John	It sounds like you kept pretty busy.
Kelly	There was a lot to see, but we made sure to leave room for a few beach days in our schedule.
John	It must be hard to come back to the office after a trip like that.
Kelly	A little bit, but I have to earn money for my next vacation.
John	Good point! I should start saving up for a vacation, too.

Questions

1. Who do you think enjoyed their vacation more?

2. Do you think Kelly should have relaxed more on her vacation?

3. Do you think Kelly enjoys traveling? Why?

4. What do you talk about with coworkers after a vacation?

The Highlight of My Trip

Top 10 Countries for Tourism

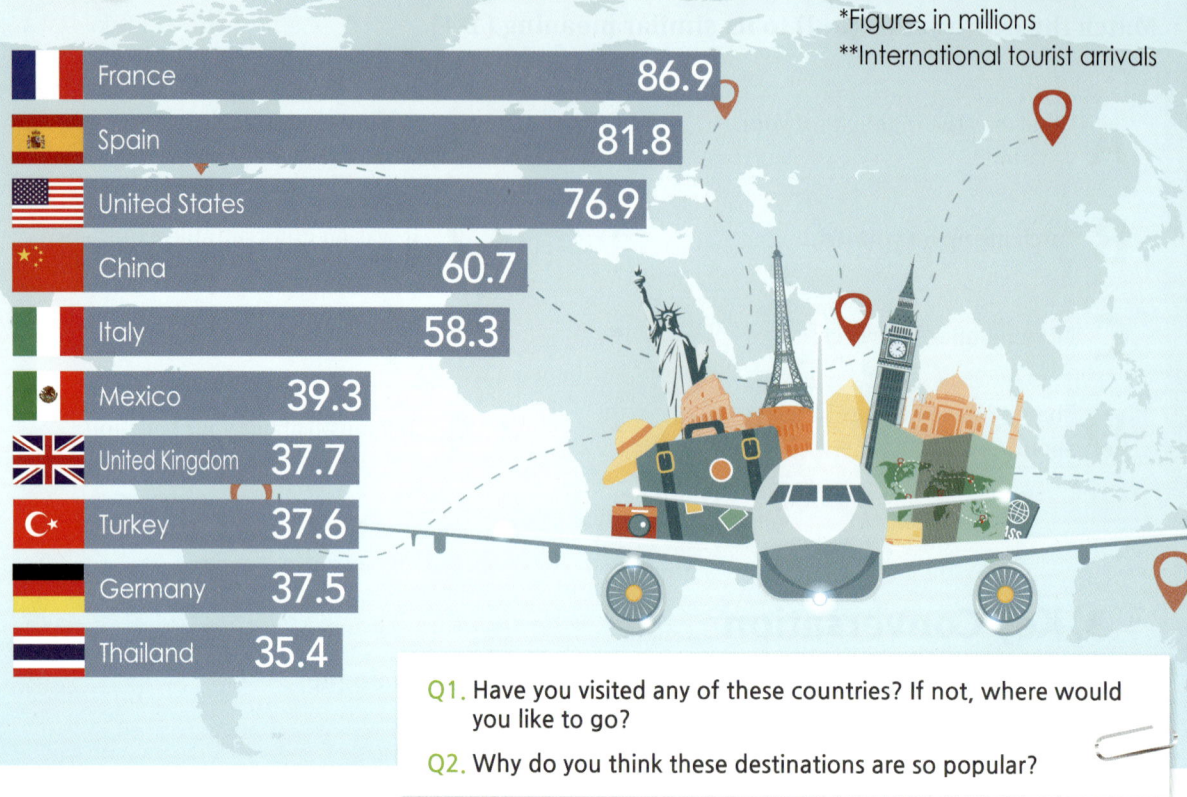

*Figures in millions
**International tourist arrivals

🇫🇷	France	86.9
🇪🇸	Spain	81.8
🇺🇸	United States	76.9
🇨🇳	China	60.7
🇮🇹	Italy	58.3
🇲🇽	Mexico	39.3
🇬🇧	United Kingdom	37.7
🇹🇷	Turkey	37.6
🇩🇪	Germany	37.5
🇹🇭	Thailand	35.4

Q1. Have you visited any of these countries? If not, where would you like to go?

Q2. Why do you think these destinations are so popular?

4. Language Practice

Using the key words, complete the sentences then practice making your own sentences.

Practice #1 — Special moments

- looking around
- taking / class
- visiting / temple

★ My favorite moment was _____ an ancient _____.

★ The highlight of the trip for me was _____ the national art museum.

★ The thing I enjoyed most was _____ a cooking _____.

Practice #2 — Discussing itineraries

- three days
- moved on
- as a base

★ We used Prague _____ for taking tours to nearby cities.

★ After visiting Paris, we _____ to Brussels.

★ We stayed in Lisbon for _____.

Practice #3 — Inconveniences

- the food
- jetlag
- got lost

★ On the second day, we _____ for hours.

★ I enjoyed everything but _____.

★ Once we got over _____, everything was easy.

5. Role Plays

Look at the situations and act out the role plays with your partner.

Situation #1

Role A
Your friend just came back from a vacation in Europe. You haven't talked to your friend in a while and can't remember exactly where he or she planned to go. Make conversation with him or her about the trip.

1. Ask your friend how the trip was.
2. Ask your friend where he or she went.
3. Ask what his or her favorite part of the trip was.

Role B
You are meeting your friend after an amazing two-week trip to Europe. You traveled to London, Paris, and Barcelona. Your favorite thing was the museums in Paris. You especially enjoyed visiting the Louvre to see famous artworks. Tell your friend about your experiences.

1. Tell your friend how much you enjoyed the trip.
2. Explain where you went.
3. Tell about the highlight of your trip.

Role A
A foreign friend is visiting you. He or she wants to travel to another city while you are working this week. Give your friend advice on good places to visit that are easy to reach from your city. Ask questions to determine a location to recommend.

1. Ask what kinds of things your friend wants to see.
2. Ask how your friend would like to travel.
3. Recommend somewhere for your friend to visit.

Role B
You have traveled abroad to visit a friend. Your friend is busy with work during the week, so you want to take a short trip to see another part of the country for two or three days. Ask your friend to recommend a small city for you to visit that has historical sites. You would prefer to travel by train, but you don't mind taking the bus. You'd like to spend less than 3 hours traveling each way.

1. Explain what you would like to see.
2. Tell your friend how you would like to travel.
3. Ask questions about the place your friend recommended.

Situation #2

Situational Collocations!

Look at the collocations and try making your own sentences.

pack bag	I packed my bag few hours before the flight.
tropical country	I love visiting tropical countries for their beaches.
first class	I only travel first class for business purposes.
package holiday	I went on a package holiday with my parents.
new experiences	I've made so many new experiences during my travels.
ask directions	I lost my map and had to ask directions from the locals.
travel diary	I was inspired to start writing a travel diary.
popular destination	I always visit popular destinations first.

1.
2.

The Highlight of My Trip

Quotes to Fuel Your Wanderlust

"It is not down in any map; true places never are." — Herman Melville

"Life is either a daring adventure or nothing at all." — Helen Keller

"The journey not the arrival matters." — T.S. Eliot

"To travel is to live." — Hans Christian Andersen

"I'm in love with cities I've never been to and people I've never met." — John Green

"If you think adventures are dangerous, try routine: It's lethal." — Paul Coelho

"Live life with no excuses, travel with no regret." — Oscar Wilde

"Once a year, go someplace you've never been before." — Dalai Lama

6. Cultural Discussion Questions

Talk about the questions in as much detail as possible.

1. Tell about the last trip you took. Where did you go? Who did you travel with?

2. Do you prefer to travel independently or in groups? Why?

3. If money and time were no object, where would you want to go? Why?

4. How do you choose a vacation destination? Explain your planning process.

Did You Know?

Read and discuss how you feel about each fact.

1. Did you know that **tourism** accounts for **5%** of the world's economy?

2. Did you know the first **space tourist** was US businessman Dennis Tito who was reported to have paid **$20 million** for a trip to the **International Space Station** in 2001?

the most popular types of travel

- **Weekend Getaway** - Do you want to get away from it all, but you can't afford to take time off work? Take a short trip over the weekend. Popular weekend getaway ideas include domestic travel and flying to nearby international destinations.
- **Backpacking** - It is the perfect choice for when you take several months (or even years) making your way around the world. Often backpackers travel on a tight budget with a loose itinerary.
- **Road Trip** - Buckle your seatbelt and get ready to hit the open road! Stop when you feel like it and enjoy interesting scenery out of your car window. This kind of trip is perfect for a longer affordable vacation or even a weekend getaway.
- **Event Travel** - This involves traveling to a destination to attend a specific event, such as the Olympics, the World Cup or even watching your favorite band in concert.
- **Group Tour** - No matter what your age or interests, there is a group tour out there for you. These trips are perfect when you want to relax and have someone else take care all the small details. Your itinerary will be packed with many different activities so you will never be bored.

Q. What types of travel have you tried? What was your favorite?

7. Slang & Idioms

Match the slang phrases and idioms with their definitions and use them to complete the sentences below.

1. ___ off the beaten path
2. ___ travel light
3. ___ living out of a suitcase
4. ___ itchy feet
5. ___ backseat driver

A. to stay very briefly in several places, with only the belongings in your suitcase
B. a passenger in a car who insists on giving the driver unwanted directions and advice
C. far away from where people normally live or go
D. to take little baggage
E. feeling the need to travel

1. I'm dreading taking this road trip with my brother. He's such a _____.
2. I'm on the road for three months at a time for work, so I've gotten pretty used to _____.
3. After a few months at home, she began to get _____ and started planning her next trip.
4. To avoid paying baggage fees, I always try to _____.
5. I prefer to avoid crowds by traveling to places that are _____.

Wrapping Up!

Write down four things you learned from this lesson and review.

New Get Up To Speed+ Book 3
SLANG & IDIOM GLOSSARY

Lesson 1

a spread	a large and impressively elaborate meal
could eat a horse	to be extremely hungry
eating me out of house and home	to eat so much as to deplete someone's resources
feed an army	to have a lot of food
show up empty-handed	without bringing anything

Lesson 2

carpool	an arrangement between people to make a regular journey in a single vehicle
drove a hard bargain	to be uncompromising in making a deal
for a spin	to test or try out something, especially an automobile
fully loaded	with all the options
put the pedal to the metal	to drive as fast as possible

Lesson 3

all-nighter	an event or task that continues throughout the night
call it a night	to stop what you have been doing and go home
hit the road	to have to go
hit the sack	to go to bed
split	to leave a place

Lesson 4

dog days	the hottest period of the year
dog-eat-dog	a situation in which there is fierce, ruthless competition
fighting like cats and dogs	to fight and argue a lot
let the cat out of the bag	reveal a secret carelessly or by mistake
working like a dog	to work extremely hard

Lesson 5

apple of my eye	the one you love the most
head over heels	to be madly in love
honeymoon period	a happy time at the start of a new relationship
lovebirds	an openly affectionate couple
match made in heaven	a couple who gets along perfectly

Lesson 6

make a little money on the side	to make extra money in addition to one's regular job
if money were no object	if the cost didn't matter
pay my dues	to make an official payment to an organization you belong to
taken up	to become interested or engaged in something
throw in the towel	to abandon a struggle

Lesson 7

foodie	a person who loves food and is very interested in different types of food
hit the spot	to be exactly what is required
meat-and-potatoes	ordinary but fundamental things; basic ingredients
picky eater	a person who is selective about what he or she eats
totally stuffed	to have consumed food in such a large quantity that you feel very full

Lesson 8

catch up on lost sleep	to make up sleep that you missed earlier
running errands	to go out to buy or do something
take it easy	to relax and rest
TGIF	an acronym for "Thank God It's Friday"
went out for brunch	to eat a late morning meal

Lesson 9

break the news	tell someone something they did not expect or bad news
double-booked	to have scheduled two things at a conflicting time
push back	to delay
running behind schedule	to do something later than planned
something came up	something unexpected happened

Lesson 10

go broke	to no longer have money
highway robbery	excessive profit from a business transaction
living hand to mouth	to barely make enough to pay one's living expenses
pay off	to pay (a debt or a creditor) in full
skyrocketed	to rise extremely quickly

Lesson 11

green around the gills	sickly-looking
on the mend	improving in health or condition; recovering
picture of health	to appear very healthy
sick in bed	remaining in bed while one is ill
went under the knife	to undergo surgery

Lesson 12

backseat driver	a passenger in a car who insists on giving the driver unwanted directions and advice
itchy feet	feeling the need to travel
living out of a suitcase	to stay very briefly in several places, with only the belongings in your suitcase
off the beaten path	far away from where people normally live or go
travel light	to take little baggage

New Get Up To Speed+ Book 3
ANSWER KEY

Lesson 1

Useful Expressions

a 3
b 4
c 1
d 2

Language Practice

Practice #1
★ after work
★ next weekend
★ Saturday night

Practice #2
★ getting together
★ come over for dinner
★ having a bite

Practice #3
★ six o'clock
★ around 9
★ half past five

Slang & Idioms

1 E a spread
2 A eating me out of house and home
3 C could eat a horse
4 B feed an army
5 D show up empty-handed

Lesson 2

Useful Expressions

a 3
b 4
c 1
d 2

Language Practice

Practice #1
★ customize / interior
★ GPS
★ rearview camera

Practice #2
★ gas mileage
★ air conditioning
★ manual transmission

Practice #3
★ cut a deal
★ give a discount
★ any extras

Slang & Idioms

1 D drove a hard bargain
2 C fully loaded
3 A put the pedal to the metal
4 E for a spin
5 B carpool

Lesson 3

Useful Expressions

a 4
b 1
c 3
d 2

Language Practice

Practice #1
★ head for home or take off
★ all
★ all

Practice #2
★ all
★ all
★ all

Practice #3

- ★ No worries. or Go sleep it off.
- ★ make it up to me
- ★ No worries. or Go sleep it off.

Slang & Idioms

1	A	all-nighter
2	D	call it a night
3	B	hit the road
4	E	split
5	C	hit the sack

Lesson 4

Useful Expressions

a   2
b   4
c   1
d   3

Language Practice

Practice #1
- ★ temperament
- ★ size
- ★ breeds

Practice #2
- ★ health issues
- ★ exercise
- ★ feed

Practice #3
- ★ independent / work late
- ★ low maintenance / busy schedule
- ★ relatively quiet / apartment

Slang & Idioms

1	C	dog-eat-dog
2	A	fighting like cats and dogs
3	B	let the cat out of the bag
4	E	dog days
5	D	working like a dog

Lesson 5

Useful Expressions

a   2
b   1
c   4
d   3

Language Practice

Practice #1
- ★ all
- ★ all
- ★ all

Practice #2
- ★ union
- ★ marriage
- ★ the start of your life together

Practice #3
- ★ belated gift
- ★ present
- ★ money

Slang & Idioms

1	B	lovebirds
2	E	match made in heaven
3	A	honeymoon period
4	D	head over heels
5	C	apple of my eye

Lesson 6

Useful Expressions

a   3
b   2
c   4
d   1

Language Practice

Practice #1

New Get Up To Speed+ Book 3
ANSWER KEY

- Didn't know / golf
- never would have guessed / kickboxing
- surprised to hear / knitting

Practice #2
- activities / spare time
- clubs / these days
- hobbies / packed schedule

Practice #3
- making jewelry / summer
- collecting coins / I was a kid
- ice skating / three years

Slang & Idioms

1	D	make a little money on the side
2	E	pay my dues
3	A	throw in the towel
4	B	taken up
5	C	if money were no object

Lesson 7

Useful Expressions

a	4
b	2
c	1
d	3

Language Practice

Practice #1
- go for or recommend
- give / a try
- go for or recommend

Practice #2
- get the dressing on the side
- substitute steamed veggies
- stay away from / shrimp

Practice #3
- suggest / order
- recommend here
- get today

Slang & Idioms

1	D	meat-and-potatoes
2	E	foodie
3	A	hit the spot
4	B	picky eater
5	C	totally stuffed

Lesson 8

Useful Expressions

a	1
b	4
c	2
d	3

Language Practice

Practice #1
- Why did you have to work?
- What did you see?
- What movie did you watch?

Practice #2
- deep cleaned my apartment / weekend
- played soccer / Sunday afternoon
- went for a hike / Saturday

Practice #3
- attended church / Sunday morning
- worked on the project report / over the weekend
- had a few beers / last Saturday

Slang & Idioms

1	E	catch up on lost sleep
2	A	take it easy
3	D	TGIF
4	C	running errands

5	B	went out for brunch

c	1
d	3

Language Practice

Practice #1
- rent / $950
- phone / $80
- electricity / $50

Practice #2
- cable or landline
- water
- cable or landline

Practice #3
- direct debit
- online or over the phone
- online or over the phone

Slang & Idioms

1	D	highway robbery
2	E	skyrocketed
3	B	pay off
4	A	living hand to mouth
5	C	go broke

Lesson 9

Useful Expressions

a	4
b	1
c	2
d	3

Language Practice

Practice #1
- cancel / appointment
- rescheduling / meeting
- came up / make it to

Practice #2
- give 24 hours' notice / cancel the appointment
- no problem / reschedule
- meeting / pushed back

Practice #3
- take a rain check / do it another day
- come up / need to cancel
- running late / Go ahead

Slang & Idioms

1	D	break the news
2	A	push back
3	E	running behind schedule
4	B	something came up
5	C	double-booked

Lesson 10

Useful Expressions

a	2
b	4

Lesson 11

Useful Expressions

a	3
b	4
c	1
d	2

Language Practice

Practice #1
- your migraine
- the pain in your shoulder
- a fever

New Get Up To Speed+ Book 3
ANSWER KEY

Practice #2
★ undergo surgery
★ follow this treatment
★ was hospitalized

Practice #3
★ write a prescription
★ draw blood
★ make a diagnosis

Slang & Idioms
1	C	went under the knife
2	E	on the mend
3	D	picture of health
4	A	sick in bed
5	B	green around the gills

Slang & Idioms
1	C	backseat driver
2	D	living out of a suitcase
3	A	itchy feet
4	E	travel light
5	B	off the beaten path

Lesson 12

Useful Expressions
a	1
b	4
c	2
d	3

Language Practice

Practice #1
★ visiting / temple
★ looking around
★ taking / class

Practice #2
★ as a base
★ moved on
★ three days

Practice #3
★ got lost
★ the food
★ jetlag